THE CHEEKY GUIDE TO BRIGHTON

The Cheeky Guide To Brighton

by David Bramwell, Alessandra Berardi & Jeremy Plotnikoff

ISBN 0 9536110 0 0

Published in 1999 by
Cheeky Chops Publishing
72 Buckingham Rd
Brighton BN1 3RJ
Email: us@cheeky-chops.freeserve.co.uk

Thanks to Freddie from Scene 22, Kieran, James from G-Scene, Dominic from Coopers Cask, Jem from Baggies and Lady Laverne for giving up their fag breaks and answering a load of dumb questions.

Special thanks to Stella and Anthony for their illustrations, and Martin for the velvet suit story.

Apologies to Sue Nichols for misplacing her email on Gay Pride and if it's any consolation we all slept badly that night.

Cover illustrations and much more by the very lovely Lisa Holdcroft. Contact 705658.

Cover design and help with layout by Peter Pavement.

Printed in Great Britain by Midas Printing, London.

THE CHEEKY GUIDE TO BRIGHTON

CHEEKY CHOPS PUBLICATIONS

About this Book

ALEX AND I MET in the Phoenix gallery a few years ago, looking for her false teeth. I joined in the search and we somehow ended up in bed together. I have always secretly wondered how many other men she ensnared this way. Three years later Jeremy moved in round the corner. We met him in the street one day looking for somewhere to buy milk. I suggested the shop round the corner but he said: *'Look, wouldn't it just be easier if we wrote a guide, save this sort of thing happening again?'*

So it was decided. The three of us set off around Brighton, with Alex and Jeremy on top holding the reins. We soon established our roles – I was picked to write it because of some Booker Prize I once won, while Jeremy and Alex did everything else. When it was almost done, we locked ourselves away for a month to get it all finished, and it was all they could do to stop me from galloping around the room and eating the final proofs. It was around this time that I first started to suspect that I was a horse.

The Creators:

David Bramwell (author) moved to Brighton in 1991 after realising that Coventry is not all it's cracked up to be. He is known by tens of people and is particularly loved for his quirky charm of butting in when someone is talking. He is Brighton's current reigning wrestling champion and by sheer coincidence is married to Alex, the editor of this book. Inspired by Beckham and Posh Spice, they have a new baby daughter called Skegness.

Jeremy Plotnikoff (production, marketing and graphics) was washed up on Brighton beach after a particularly heavy drinking binge in Glasgow. Russian in origin, Jeremy is loved for his naturally furry head and body. Yet to have grasped any of the English language since his recent arrival in Brighton 9 years ago, he communicates through grunts and strange wheezing noises, but was recently discovered just to have been choking on a biscuit.

Alex (editor) is a local legend for having single-handedly swum the channel just to get someone's frisbee back. Her favourite item is her black PVC catsuit which she always wears at fancy dress parties, even if the theme is Mexican. She collects dead sea-gulls and is currently knitting them into an enormous scarf for her idol, Patrick Swayze.

In researching this book we have:

▸ had ectoplasm thrown at us
▸ nearly died after an encounter with the world's worst halitosis
▸ met the ghost of my dead grandfather
▸ given up trying to review a comic shop when it became apparent that their game of dungeons and dragons stopped for no-one
▸ auditioned lap-dancing girls
▸ been fondled in a séance
▸ found a baby wallaby in the High Street
▸ been subjected to half an hour of Bavarian oompah music
▸ witnessed a guy walk in a café, eat a bowl of sugar, shout — 'fuck the lot of you, I'm going home for a wank.' And then walk out again
▸ And Jeremy fell in love.

We have toiled day and night to be accurate with prices, times of opening etc, but we're only human (except Jeremy who's Canadian) and things change quickly in Brighton, a café today could be an airport tomorrow. If you spot any changes or mistakes, drop us a line and we'll be grateful. Gushing adoration in the form of gifts and money will also be warmly received.

Nobody paid to be reviewed in this book and with the exception of a cookie and half a Guinness, we haven't had any freebies.

I know, I know, what a wasted opportunity.

The Cheeky Guide to Brighton

Introduction

In the beginning there was only herring

1500's Brighton starts life as a prosperous fishing village, paying the government 4000 herring a year in taxes.

1783 The town becomes a fashionable health resort when a certain Doctor Russell declared that drinking the sea water here would get rid of your boils and put hair on your chest. Not advisable today unless you want to get rid of your hair and have boils on your chest instead.

1823 The Prince Regent has the Royal Pavilion built as somewhere he can bring back a few mates after the pubs had closed.

1930's Torsos start turning up in boxes around the town beginning the reign of the infamous 'trunk murders'. The King's elephant was suspected but nothing was ever proved.

1960's Brighton is host to the 1964 'It's a knockout', featuring the Mods and Rockers fighting it out on the seafront. The town remains a regular host to holiday battles for the next few years or so, as the beach becomes no mans land, and whoever takes control of the novelty postcard shop is the winner.

1972 Sir Laurence Olivier campaigns fiercely for kippers to be returned to the menu on the Brighton Belle railway line.

1974 Singer David Lee Roth re-locates to Brighton after quitting his band 'The Red Ball Jets' and opens an unsuccessful sandwich shop called 'Roth and Rolls'. A year later he returned to LA and formed the legendary Van Halen.

1979 Quadrophenia is released and Sting has his equity card revoked. Scuffles start up again on the beaches for a while, as all the Mods completely miss the point of the movie.

1984 Lady Thatcher visits the bathroom and survives the IRA bombing of The Grand Hotel. Others are not so lucky.

1988   Brighton witnesses its first cannabis famine as infamous ex-resident Howard Marks is arrested.

1989   Hundreds of packets of cocaine are found washed up on the beach, up the road at Peacehaven. Police cordon off the area when Bobby Gillespie arrives to have a closer look.

1995   The West Pier is declared an independent state by a bunch of squatters on the West pier (but after two weeks they run out of rizlas). Obviously inspired by this, only a few months later, Chris Eubank announces in the press that he wants to buy the West Pier, and set up his home there, with a helicopter pad at the end.

1998   A chip-pan fire causes the famous Albion Hotel on the seafront to burn down. *'Meester Fawlty, is fire is fire....'*

1999   The *Cheeky Guide to Brighton* is finally published, despite several death threats and a kidnap attempt by their arch-enemy-'The Flaccid Guide to Brighton'.

Brighton Urban Myths

HIPPY STUFF

New Age legend decrees that a stone circle once stood in the Old Steine, but was smashed up by the Victorians and used to form the base of the big fountain there. This is acclaimed as the magnet of all Brighton's energy and weirdness. It is interesting to note that Old Steine means 'old stone'. Give Julian Cope a ring, he'll put you straight.

GRAVE TALES

Brighton seems particularly rich in stories of underground tunnels and burial chambers, and one particular myth tells of a house here in Orange Row, which is supposed to have the original entrance to the old Brighton catacombs. Although blocked off with railway girders now, it is said to be still littered with the dead bodies from an ancient flu epidemic.

Also, keep your eyes peeled for the pyramid-shaped grave of a guy called Mad Jack, who insisted on being buried sitting at a table, with his dinner in front of him. And where else would the world's most infamous occultist, Aleister Crowley, be cremated, other than our very own Woodvale Cemetery?

MURDER MYSTERY

Take one of the tours during the festival and you will learn about some of the gruesome murders that happened in the 20s and 30s here. There are many accounts of body parts being left around town in trunks, and a severed head is said to have once been left in a bag by the Horse and Groom bar in Hanover.

One year, Jason, a friend of mine, decided to do the murder tour, and left his house to walk down to Bartholomew Square where it was starting. The guide introduced the tour by saying-

'We'll commence by visiting the location of probably the most gruesome murder Brighton has ever known.' and proceeded to walk the group back to Margaret Street, where Jason lived.

'Hey this is the street where I live!' he thought with growing alarm.

'And it was in this house that the body was dismembered and stored in a cupboard for two weeks...' said the guide pointing at Jason's bedroom window.

Jason always sleeps with the light on now and has rekindled his friendship with Mr Floppy his big fluffy bunny.

How to get Here

BY RAIL

Trains from London leave Victoria and Kings Cross Thames Link about twice an hour. The Victoria link is usually quicker: about 50 minutes for the fast train. Be careful when returning to London late at night however, check when the last train leaves, it's usually before 12am, even at weekends. There are also direct train services along the coast if you are not coming via London.

At the station

You'll find cash-machines, bureau de change, hotel reservation kiosk and buses and taxis waiting outside. If all that seems too formal, just go straight out, keep walking and you'll be at the beach in less than 10 minutes.

SUNDAY TRAINS

For some reason, there are often repairs to the tracks on a Sunday, which means your inward or outward journey to London may involve three coach journeys via Littlehampton and Barnsley, so check before you travel. I kid you not, I have spent some miserable Sunday evenings dreaming of being at home by the fire sipping fine wines, when instead I'm standing in the rain in the middle of sodding nowhere, waiting for a BR bus driven by some fuckwit who doesn't know where he's taking you. And when he does eventually arrive an hour later and sets off, the bloody bus breaks down. And to cop it all you don't have a seat. And yes this has happened to me before. Now that's off my chest I feel much better. Ignore this at your peril.

Rail Enquiries
0345 484950

BY PLANE

From Gatwick A train will get you to Brighton in half an hour. If there are four of you a taxi will probably cost less because the trains are so damned expensive here. The cheapest option is to get a coach.

From Heathrow What a drag, you must really enjoy doing things the hard way. Get a tube to Victoria then a train from there. It'll take two hours at the most.

BY COACH

National Express
Corner of St. James's Street and Old Steine
FOR NATIONAL EXPRESS ENQUIRIES: 0990 808080

To travel between Brighton and London costs £8 for a single day return and takes about an hour

BY ROAD

Once you've packed your sandwiches, toothbrush, bucket and spade, make your way to the London orbital M25 then take the M23/A23 all the way to Brighton. It shouldn't take more than forty-five minutes once you've left the M25. It's as simple as that. If you travel between 5pm and 7pm through the London rush-hour, it's best to take a travel scrabble. If you're lucky enough not to be coming via London you'll probably be taking the coastal route along the A27.

PARKING

Devilishly tricky and expensive. If you're not parking in a multi-storey you'll need vouchers from newsagents and any other shops with a green 'v' outside for parking in the streets. It's a little confusing because it looks the same as the vegetarian 'v' that you get on Linda McCartney sausages. My advice is park out of town and walk or get a bus, it's never that far to anywhere in Brighton. Voucher parking starts at £1 an hour in the town centre and 50p outside. One of the cheapest car-parks is near the bottom of Trafalgar Street.

BY HELICOPTER
FOR SHOREHAM AIRPORT ENQUIRIES: (01273) 452304

You'll get as far as Shoreham airport, then it's a 2 hour walk to Brighton along the seafront. What do you mean you haven't got a helicopter? Everyone in Brighton's got one.

Getting Around

TAXIS

202020 • 204060 • 747474 • 205205

There are plenty to choose from and all the services are pretty much the same. It shouldn't cost more than a few quid to get across town and I believe all the companies are 24-hour. Incidentally, the taxi-drivers in Brighton are required by law to carry inflatable rings under their seats so check when you get in. If there isn't one you should be able to blag a free ride.

LIMOS

If you want to do the tourist thing you could always take a trip in Brighton's stretch limo, although parading around in a small white whale at £50 an hour isn't my idea of money well spent.

Hannington's Limos
(01273) 329877

Linkline Limos
(01273) 580500

Lancaster Limos
0800 7313613 • (01273) 886200

BUSES

For getting around the town centre there is a flat fare of 70p. Buses are frequent and will take you practically anywhere.

BUS TOURS

Open-Topped Bus Tour
(01273) 746205
Brighton for lazy-bones. Do the lot in one hour for £6.50.

The tour operates March to October and there are spots all over town where you can catch a bus, the most obvious being outside the Palace Pier. The tour is conducted in over 20 languages including Esperanto.

FESTIVAL TOURS

During the festival in May there are a whole host of tours ranging from ghost tours, gay tours, historical tours, literary tours and a tour of the sewers. Some are good, some are awfully dull.

The sewers tour is particularly good and I can never resist buying something from the souvenir shop.

Some of the ghost tours are fun too as you always get a few

good stories to take away, even if they are made up.

I've always wanted to remember some of the scary places I've been taken on a midnight tour, then the next evening dress up and hide in one of the spots and jump out and scare all the tourists at an opportune moment. You're right, I have a juvenile sense of humour.

BIKES

It's quite pleasant cycling round Brighton, although the hills can be a bit of a drag at times and the council have only made a half-arsed attempt with proper cycle lanes. The seafront is great though, it's long and flat and you can play dodging the dozy gits who always walk in the cycle lanes there.

CYCLE HIRE

SUNRISE CYCLE HIRE
(01273) 748881 (late March-November) under the West Pier

Three quid an hour, twelve quid a day, ten if you're a student. They also do tandems which is handy if you're a horse like me needing to make a fast getaway from the scene of a crime.

Oh my god, have I said too much?

PLANET CYCLE HIRE
Madeira Drive, opposite the Anchor (01273) 695755
Mon-Sat 10am-6pm

The same as sunrise but open all year round.

SKATEBOARDING

Brighton has one of the largest collections of skateboarders in England. This probably has as much to do with the weather as anything else, but we also have our own skate park and numerous other good spots to skate. These are however diminishing rapidly, as lippy young ankle-biters with bad attitude have pissed off the general public so much that £150 fines are starting to be issued against skaters.

The Skatepark
Located at the Level

The park consists of one halfpipe and numerous other small ramps, and it is a good place to meet other skaters.

There are good displays of local graffiti here, just take a peek on the back of the halfpipe.

Other Places Include:

St. George's statue

(Old Steine)

There are some nice ledges here

Cottesmore School

Couple of good flat banks

Woolworths

Some cool places behind here

Seafront (Between the piers)

has some good drops and rails.

Sainsburys

The car park is a good place to skate if it is raining (only after shop hours). Don't abuse this, they are OK about skating here at night, but they are not cool about it when the shop is open.

WALKING

Visitors from LA might be interested to learn that this outdated form of transport is still immensely popular in Brighton.

Here and There Everywhere

THE OLD LANES

A series of wonderfully confusing narrow passages and cobbled streets make up this part of Brighton, which is steeped in history and full of stories of smugglers, ghosts and randy nuns.

The passages are known locally as twittens, (an old smugglers' expression meaning 'thin street with over-priced shops') and are enclosed by West Street, East Street and the seafront.

You should enjoy simply wandering around here, but don't worry if you get lost, I still do and I used to work here. To find the centre of the maze, try and locate the dolphin statues in the fountain at Brighton Square. It is customary to throw the guidebook into the fountain here and make a wish. If you head off past Rounder

Records, have a look at their back wall to see which album they have spray-painted on it. As a reference point, you'll be on your way back to East Street.

Although this is an area reputedly only famous for jewellery and antiques, there is also an abundance of cafés, restaurants and clothes shops. It feels much more antiquated compared to the fashionable North Laines but at night time the busy restaurants give it a new lease of life.

The best time to visit the Old Lanes is at dawn, when the noise of the seagulls and the strange light of early morning pierce through the empty alleyways. At times like this, eerie folklore tales about ghosts and ghoulish fishermen no longer seem like a load of old cobblers.

19

If you haven't got long in Brighton, I'd recommend a mooch around here. Try Food For Friends for lunch, and make sure you poke your head in at Fabrica (opposite the post office on Ship St) to see what dazzling art installation they have in this beautiful building.

If it's summer, this is a busy area for busking. Look out for the old guy who busks with a rabbit. Once I even saw a girl busking with a rat here. She kept it on her shoulder whilst playing her guitar, and now and again she let it drink out of her mouth. **EUURRGGHH!**

NORTH LAINES

Known as Brighton's bohemian quarters, this unmissable area has some of the best shops, pubs and cafés in town. Glamorous, young, posy, vibrant, and pretentious it may be, but Cleethorpes High Street it is not. In fact, the North Laines does its best to be Haight Ashbury, Carnaby Street and Greenwich Village, all rolled into a handful of streets.

UNIQUE THINGS ABOUT THE NORTH LAINES

1) Smoking is compulsory in most bars and cafes in the North Laines.
2) Everyone who lives here must pay £10 a year to a man known as Dave Suit.
3) If your parents turn up wearing pringle jumpers, somebody will see it as an important fashion statement.

This locality prides itself on its café culture, which blossoms during the summer months. Balconies heave with milkshakes and suntanned legs, and tables and chairs start to sprawl out onto the roads. It's a pleasure just to hang out on some of the café balconies and watch the world and its dog go by. The Grinder and Kensingtons are notably good haunts for this. On Saturdays, Gardner Street is pedestrianised, and becomes one enormous mass of cappuccinos and sunglasses.

The North Laines is of course posers' paradise, and from 60s kitsch to 90s chic, every fashion gets a look in. Walk down Kensington Gardens in full 'KISS' make-up with cream crackers stuck to you, and still few heads will turn.

Many of the shops here are unique and shamelessly glitzy. Pussy, Revolución, Borderline and Re-vamp are just a few worth seeking out, where you will find everything from wrestling masks to silver platforms and fetish kitchen-ware. This area has a fabulous collection of record shops and clothes shops too, not to mention retro gear from the likes of Dolly and Nice 'n' Easy. And don't be afraid to stray off the beaten track at times, Acme Art with its surreal sculptures and eccentric owner is well worth seeking out.

"If you stand in the same spot for too long in Sydney Street, someone will stick a poster on you"

The shops are also a good starting point for checking out what's going on in the clubs and venues, as the streets visibly sag under the weight of posters and fliers in every window. In fact, it can be information overload as they are handed to you on street corners and thrown at you from the tops of buildings. You'll even find them taped to the pavement at weekends.

In the North Laines anything goes, the more flamboyant the better. Fashions and sub-cultures fight for space along these busy streets, so don't be surprised if you end up going home with an exotic tattoo and your genitals pierced, it will simply have been a Brighton experience.

The Beach

Stretching from the nudist beach near the Marina across to Hove and beyond, this is one of the main inspirations behind all that is Brighton. In summer it's always littered with life, from families with kids to groups of bright young things, and the obligatory loony with a metal detector.

'Hey I found another ring-pull'

When the sun is out, most likely you'll want to join the crowds down there and brave the sea for a swim, or just hang out and be a sun-lizard. There's also a new volleyball area if you like to do it Baywatch style, or for the more adventurous, the banana boat ride is definitely worth trying.

At night, between the two piers, the beach is usually crowded with overspill from The Fortune of War and other bars down there, and there's usually a good buzz about the place. This is also a hot-spot for many of the best clubs, like the Zap, The Honey Club and The Beach, so expect the clubbing crowd to be out in force. It's definitely a good place to hang out and chat, and if you feel like doing a little wooing, it can be a lot more conducive outside than in, where you'll have to shout and slobber in someone's ear just to tell them you like their friend.

Sometimes though, when it's a warm night and you're in the mood, it's good to by-pass the busy bars and clubs. Just find a quiet spot, get some beers and food, and come here with friends and watch the sun going down.

If you're still around after all the clubs have cleared, it eventually gets pretty empty, although there's always the odd clubber who's crashed out after too many pills, and a guy still looking for his contact lens. In fact, even in the cruellest winters you will find little pockets of life here, like penguins on an iceberg. What better than a walk by the sea for a little thinking and introspection?

And finally, it's time to come clean. Yes, it's true I'm afraid, it is all stones and not sand. But as a small compensation, when you take your picnic down the beach, and the wind whips up, you will not be crunching your way through a cheese sandwich. Saying that, over 4 billion stones and not one decent one for skimming...

The Seafront

WEST OF THE PALACE PIER

"The beach washes away the ills of mankind."
Dr Richard Russell

If you don't have a lot of time to spend in Brighton, you should definitely make a priority of visiting the seafront between the Palace Pier and The West Pier. Here you'll find cafés, plenty of clubs, amusement arcades, The Fishing Museum, artists at work, palmists, sculptures on the beach and usually an assortment of outdoor entertainment during summer. When it's warm, the beach here just packs out, and you can sit outside the café-bars or bring your own food and beer and find your own spot on the beach. (A deck chair for the afternoon will cost you a quid). If you want a good walk, follow the seafront path all the way to the multi-coloured beach huts.

The Palace Pier

For information call 50935

Our number one attraction. Brighton without a visit to the pier is like Tommy Cooper without the fez. Throw all caution to the wind and indulge in a bit of cheesy seaside fun.

Choose the pier, choose the 2 penny falls, choose to feed the seagulls, choose fish and chips, Belgian waffles, a kebab from the Taj Mahal, choose to have your palm read by gypsy Jim the Australian mystic, choose a cuddly Garfield by shooting at the plastic ducks, choose to sing 'I Did It My Way' in front of blokes with streaked hair at the Karaoke bar, choose different coloured sticks of rock for your mates at work, choose the dodgems, the dolphin derby, go on the ghost ride on your own to prove that you're not scared of the dark, choose to listen to some guy say 'three swings of the hammer could win you a big red dog' over and over again, choose to go on the Helter Skelter because you're feeling like a big kid, choose to tell the pier DJ to stop playing bloody Mike and the Mechanics records. I chose something else. I chose to stay indoors and write a book.

#1 helter skelter   #2 seagull   #3 clairvoyant   #4 karaoke singers   #5 ice cream

Pierspotting

There are dozens of places to stop for food. Most of the clubs do refreshments in the afternoons, which gives you a chance to check out what they're like inside. If you want to leave some of the crowds behind though, wait until you reach the sci-fi looking Al Fresco or The Meeting Place café (near the angel statue), it's much more civilised.

THINGS TO LOOK OUT FOR

The Victorian Penny Arcades

There are two between the piers, where for 50p you get 5 old Victorian pennies to use on all the old machines. I particularly like the 'What The Butler Saw' machines, especially – 'Two Lovely Ladies' and 'Easy Chair Frolics'. Then there's the 'Win A Fag' machine, the Electric Tickler which gives you a pleasant electric shock and all the fortune telling machines that will massage your ego.

The Big Green Bagel

This sculpture arrived about 3 years ago as a gift from the Mayor of Naples after we donated his town a large bronze herring.

Officially entitled 'Il Grande Bagel Verde', but known locally as the 'Seasick Doughnut', it survived last year's storm and several assassination attempts by local art puritans.

The Artists Quarters

This area starts just past The Big Green Bagel and is a series of interesting, tiny studios and rooms set under the arches of the promenade where painters, sculptors and toy makers sell their wares. Some of the stuff is pretty unusual (like the cow paintings and puppets) and it's pleasant to wander down there on a Sunday, marvelling at how bloody talented some people are.

The West Pier

Closed until 2002 when, after extensive renovation, it will finally be re-opened to the public. But for now they're running regular tours.

EAST OF THE PALACE PIER

The miniature Volks Railway runs along this stretch of the seafront all the way to the Marina, a reminder of how much smaller people were in the old days.

Look out Blackpool

There isn't much in the way of entertainment along this stretch, unless you count two crazy golf courses and the rather shabby Peter Pan's Amusements half way down, with a few go-karts, a slide and the rather embarrassing Safari Train. Just after this however, look out for the strange old house set

into the promenade just before Duke's Mound.

The story goes that before the promenade was built, all the houses along the front were sold and demolished apart from one stubborn guy who refused to sell. The council couldn't move him, so in desperation they built the promenade over his house and it still remains there today. Clarence Palmer who owns the Volks Railway lives there now.

Further on from here is the once controversial nudist beach, which is now mainly used by the gay community.

This whole area of the seafront is in need of re-juvenation* but it does come alive when there are car rallies or events like the dance day when it fills with happy people. And finally our thought for the day: *Why does the train on the Volks Railway have a steering wheel ?*

*By that I do not mean another load of cafés and clubs. Why can't we just have some greenery along the seafront?

Aliens land in the volleyball court

KEMPTOWN

Cross over the Old Steine from the bottom of North Street and you'll find yourself in Kemptown, a haven of B&Bs, and home to much of Brighton's flourishing gay and lesbian community.

Bristling with life, day and night, Kemptown's energy seems to come from an ever-growing gay scene determined to celebrate its achievements, mixed with the overspill of all that life and vitality emanating from the seafront.

This is also a place where many of Brighton's eccentrics seem to congregate and make up for lost time. Buy your strawberries next to a drag queen in Safeway or stumble across the guy in St. James's Street who always dresses immaculately in tails and white gloves. Kemptown may not be a part of Brighton that has been dressed up for visitors, but it is precisely the rough edges that provide the appeal.

To explore Kemptown you could do worse than simply taking a walk up St. James's Street. The side streets that run down to the sea are mostly home to endless B&Bs, while the streets on the opposite side are worth investigating for the occasional curiosities, especially George Street, home to the fetish shop Kentucky Woman.

St. James's Street is also host to plenty of health food shops, second hand shops, barbers, a few good pubs and plenty of gay haunts and cruising spots. The big pink flea market deserves a visit, and look out for Jackson's on Manchester Street, decorated with bald heads and cartoons (drawn by our very own Cool Cheese).

Follow St. James's Street for long enough until eventually it becomes St. Georges Road. Here Kemptown begins to feel more like a village. Continue far enough and, at the end, you'll reach Sussex Square and Lewes Crescent. These stunning white Regency flats are occupied by some of Brighton's affluent bohemians, and have had their fair share of well-known residents, Lewis Carroll and Howard Marks being just two.

And your final Kemptown destination must surely be the first floor balcony flat of number 10 Lewes Crescent. Still regularly photographed by metal fans, this is said to be the actual room where living legend Ozzy Ozborne wrote the rock anthem 'Paranoid'.

HIGH STREET

This starts as North Street down at the Old Steine then becomes Western Road past the Clock Tower and once you reach Church Street, you're well into Hove.

With the exception of Ann Summers, the pound shop and some good bookshops, it's just a regular High Street with all the usual big chains and a big indoor Shopping Centre. Past Waitrose you get to see the big Regency squares, which are beautiful but the view is still much better from the seafront.

Continue for another half a mile and you will soon be deep into Hove. Tattoos and piercings start to thin out, and begin to be replaced by blue rinse hair. From here it all descends into a wilderness of restaurants, cafés, and estate agents.

THE MARINA

Situated one mile to the left of the Palace Pier. I can never really get excited about the Marina, and with the exception of taking a boatride, or a walk along the breakwater, why anyone would want to come here is a mystery.

Sure there are lots of boats, a bowling alley, cinema, some shops and a McDonalds. But if this place is so exciting, why does it need to advertise an Asda and a car-park among its main attractions?

More for yuppies and Captain Birdseye.

Stunning view of the Asda car park

WEST STREET
'A collage of Ralph Lauren'
Kieran Long

Follow the trail of strong aftershave and blue-legged girls as you enter the world of amusement arcades, nightclubs, theme pubs and burger bars. One man's meat is another man's poison. Known by the police as 'little Beirut'.

PARKS & GARDENS
Queen's Park
Between Kemptown and Hanover
If you're coming from Kemptown head up Egremont Place, go through the arch and the park is immediately on your right.

This is the closest park to the town centre and is the kind of place where football games and Tai Chi lessons exist side by side. It has a small café, toilets, tennis courts, kids play area and a fairly typical small lake (which used to be a roller skating rink in the 60s).

What I particularly like though, is the way it's landscaped with gentle hills and it has these strange old monuments littered around. Best of all, it has great climbing trees and a small death slide for kids. Be sure to come back early evening when the families have gone and treat yourself to a few goes.

Preston Park

This is the largest park in Brighton located a little way down Preston Road. For starters it's a great spot for cycling, you can use their professional track at the top of the park and then race back down over the bumpy road or simply cycle around the park's perimeter. There's also a café in the middle and loads of space for big sports games.

It's a good place for a picnic, but unfortunately the ever-present noise of cars from the main road can sometimes spoil a tranquil afternoon.

Look out for the goatee beard brigade taking ultimate frisbee very seriously and try and find the Steve Ovett statue at the bottom of the park, facing the road. Remember the Alan Partridge sketch where he 'pops out' of his skimpy satin shorts? You're seconds away Steve…

The Rock Garden

Cross over the road from Preston Park and enter this beautifully sculpted garden through a small gate. Follow the twisting paths up and around past the pond all the way to the top. Leave the path and carry on up and you can see the half-deserted railway far below. It's a nice spot for a secluded smoke or maybe 1-2-3 rescue at dusk for the big kid in you.

St. Ann's Well Gardens

This small park in Hove has a scent garden and a few little intimate picnic areas. Tennis fans might like to know that if you want a free game, they don't start charging here before 10am. My favourite feature is the strange clock on a pole that overlooks the courts and bowling green; it's straight out of The Prisoner.

The Level

Found just behind St. Peter's church, this is more of a place for hanging out in summer really.

Come and give your dog some exercise whilst watching teenage boys endanger their gonads doing BMX tricks in the skateboarding park. There's a nice bit by the paddling pool area with its trellises, little kiosks and surreal bridges, but don't get too excited. It's best as a place for a game of footie or rounders.

Don't miss the fair when it comes here for two weeks at the end of April and August.

Dyke Road Cemetary
Dyke Road opposite St. Nicholas' Church

From the Clock Tower go up Dyke Rd and you'll find it on your left just after the traffic lights.

Part cemetery, part park and relatively unknown, this is a perfect spot to come and flop about, read a book, bring a picnic or do some meditation. I love it here. It's never busy and it does the job if you want to feel like you've left the rat race behind. Look out for Gandhi's grave.

The Pavilion Gardens and Café

After a morning's shopping in the North Laines, these gardens behind The Pavilion are perfect for a spot of lolling about. There's usually a ton of people about when it's warm but it has a more intimate feel than the busy beach.

If you're in need of refreshments the café does drinks and is famous for its rock cakes. Look for the photos on the café history notice board on the side of the hut. They sure had big ears in those days.

Brunswick Square Gardens

The large expanse of lawns and gardens in this stunning square are open to the public and probably would get my vote at being the best place for a picnic.

HOVE: an apology

I've probably offended quite a few people by not including Hove in the title of this book, as officially Brighton and Hove come as a package these days, but as there's not much to do there except eat and drink, it didn't seem to merit an inclusion. Hove begins at Boundary Passage (the longest alleyway in Brighton, which starts at Western Road, almost opposite Waterloo Street) and continues all the way to Devon. Having thrown off its old image of being a home for retired Tories, Hove is still primarily a residential area with a few good pubs and restaurants.

What does need to be said though, is that some of the town's most beautiful buildings can be found here, and Brunswick Square and Palmeira Square are among the finest examples of the Regency architecture this country has.

There is an old Brighton joke that Hove should be re-named 'Hove Actually', due to the countless times its residents, when asked if they live in Brighton, reply with snooty indignation – 'No, Hove actually.'

The Hemp Corporation

Hard Wearing

Easy on the Eye

Light on the Earth

**Top Quality Jeans - Dresses - Combats - Shirts - Lingerie
and much more besides
Three times stronger and more durable than cotton
Grown organically
The fullest range of hemp goods available in the U.K -
caps & hats - jewellery - bags & wallets - toiletries - food &
drink plus much more.**

**24 Church Street, Brighton
(3 minutes walk from the train station)
Office: 01273 208708
Fax: 01273 732402
Web: www.thehempcorp.demon.co.uk
Email: hempcorp@thehempcorp.demon.co.uk**

Wonderful Things To Do

COOL BUILDINGS

The Pavilion
Old Steine (01273) 290900
Open 10-5pm Oct-May,
10-6pm June-September
£4.50 adults, £2.75 children,
£3.25 concessions

If, like me, you have a pathological hatred for those dreary tours of stately homes, I still recommend a visit here. True, it's the familiar set-up with those awful little rope chains, and hordes of American tourists giving 'oohs', and 'aaahs' in every room, but you can't escape the simple fact that the Pavilion is just stunning.

With the exception of the Pier, this is Brighton's most famous landmark. Could you really visit Paris and not go up the Eiffel Tower?

Built as a weekend retreat for the Prince Regent in 1823, this extravagant palace is home to some of the most flamboyant architecture and interior design. Despite the Moorish look from the outside, the interior actually has a predominant Chinese theme. Inside it's a labyrinth of colour, bamboo, dragon sculptures and some of the most fabulous rooms I've ever set eyes on, especially the Music room.

It is well documented that the Prince was renowned for his love of women and food. In the bedroom look for the two secret doors, for his midnight rendezvous with Mrs Fitzherbert and the bloke selling seafood in a basket. One door is in a corner, the other right next to the bed. Some nights they'd both go in the wrong doors and…well you can guess the rest, but it is Brighton after all.

Don't miss the most outrageous chandelier in the Universe, bamboo trees in the kitchen, and a fire-breathing dragon. Holiday cottages do not come more exotic than this.

The TV documentary they show inside is pretty interesting, (despite the room smelling of an old people's home) and it means you don't have to waste your money on a guide book.

Dreamed-up and partly designed by the Prince Regent, this oriental pleasure palace helped establish Brighton as a fashionable place to be seen. One hundred and eighty years later, the Prince's

devotions to art, music, extravagance and indiscretion, have still left an indelible impression on the town.

The Booth Museum Of Natural History
194 Dyke Road (01273) 292777
e-mail: boothmus@pavilion.co.uk
Free entry. Bus 27/27A
Open Mon-Sat 10am-5pm
Sun 2pm-5pm Closed Thurs

This curiosity is the home to hundreds of stuffed birds, skeletons and strange things in specimen jars. When you enter you'll be struck by the smell of mothballs and how gloomy everything is. Stuffed birds tower up around you and in the centre of the room are two misplaced stained-glass windows.

At this point, if you're in a group, I recommend splitting up and going it alone for maximum effect. Walk down the aisles at the side and enter Hitchcock's terrifying world of The Birds. Down the centre you'll find jars with strange creatures in, and at the back, some impressive skeletons. If you're very lucky you might get here for a live taxidermy demonstration.

Look out for: the sheep that looks like Daisy in the Woody Allen movie, the charred remains of a (half-eaten) dodo and the rather strange 'toad in the hole'. I bet you won't find the warthog's head though.

To find the museum, follow Dyke Road from the Clock Tower and just keep walking. It'll take a good half-hour, so I'd only recommend it if you were near-by, or on bikes or something, as it's really only a twenty-minute curiosity.

Could you spend the night here on your own though? I swear they all come to life then.

Warning – check first for children's visits, they will utterly spoil your experience.

The Brighton Museum
Church Street (01273) 290800
Open Mon-Sat 10am-5pm
Sun 2-5pm Closed Wednesday

Worth a look in if you're passing, and again it's all free. If you do go, make sure you see the green gallery and the non-Western art gallery on the ground floor, they've both got interesting things like totem poles, African masks and Polynesian idols. They're particularly proud of their copy of Dali's Mae West lips sofa but no, you can't sit down and have your picture taken.

There's also loads of Regency period artefacts and an enormous painting on the stairs of the Prince Regent himself, looking like a puffed-up buffoon.

The exhibitions upstairs are generally worth a look in too, as past themes have included Fetish, Captain Beefheart paintings and Psychedelia.

If you find the skeleton under the floorboards, award yourself 3 team points.

Fabrica in the Old Lanes

The Dome Theatre
Behind the library
on Church Street

Found just behind the Pavilion, this majestic looking building used to be where the Prince Regent kept his horses. If you look carefully you can still see hoof-marks in the carpets in some places. Except you won't have the chance any more, because it's going to be closed for ages while they do a spot of much-needed renovation.

St. Bartholomews Church
Ann Street (01273) 620491

Located behind Trafalgar Street and London Road. I wouldn't go miles out of your way to come here, but if you're in the area you should pop your head around because it's kind of unusual. This is the biggest brick church in Europe and I like it because inside it's decorated with oil paintings, Italian mosaics and marble archways.

They put on a lot of concerts here too if you go in for big classical events. It could be the setting of the next Peter Greenaway film.

Fabrica
40 Duke Street (01273) 778646
Closed Dec-April due to a
lack of heating.
Open Wed-Sat 11.30am-5pm
Sun 2-5pm

Essential drop-in spot when you're in the Old Lanes, even if it's only for 2 minutes. Opposite the main post office on Ship Street, this converted church is now a gallery space with installations, contemporary art and more. It's not everyone's cup of tea but it's free, friendly and usually looks fantastic.

The Phoenix Gallery
10-14 Waterloo Place
(01273) 603700 Open Mon-Sat
11am-6pm Sun 12noon-4pm

This small gallery space is often home to some unusual and flamboyant art from local and visiting artists. Why not combine your visit with a perusal at the strange music stall that's always here at the weekend?

Also look out for the occasional gig or special event.

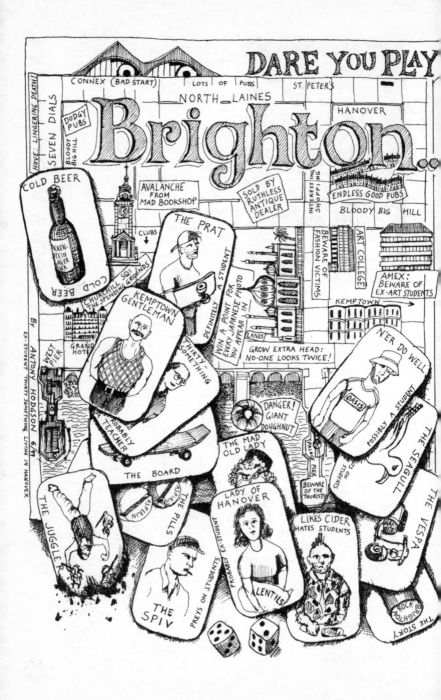

A SPOTTERS GUIDE TO BRIGHTON CELEBRITIES

What better way to spend your afternoon than going all gooey-eyed and weak-kneed at having stumbled across your favourite snooker player? Brighton is home to an eclectic bunch of celebrities and I wish you every success with your sleuthing.

CHRIS EUBANK

Easy to spot owing to the fact that most of his waking hours seem to be spent either driving his dumper truck, jeep, motorbike or tractor around the Old Lanes waving at bemused strangers.
Worth 5 points

MRS McCLUSKY
FROM GRANGE HILL

Better remembered as Bridget the Midget. I first spotted her at a Ken Campbell performance years ago and occasionally still see her at some of the more unusual theatre events.
Worth 15 points

BOBBY GILLESPIE

Recently moved to London but still pops down a lot to pick up his mail. Found at the back of gigs staggering around in the dark talking about Sun Ra and The Rolling Stones. Don't stick around too long or he'll try and smoke you.
Worth 15 Points, 20 if sober

GAZ FROM SUPERGRASS

The shy popster with the hairy face has moved to Kemptown. He can often be seen down St. James's Street with his chopper out.*
Worth 15 points

THE LEVELLERS

You'll find them in deepest Kemptown, hanging around their studio and making a racket.
Worth 10 points

EL DIABLITO

FATBOY SLIM

Best to find out where The Big Beat Boutique is on. It was at The Beach when this went to print. He'll be there DJing or snogging Zoe in the corner.
Worth 15 points

JULIE BURCHILL

Diminutive journalist with a silly voice, renowned for her opinionated codswallop. You'll find her with a coke and a smile at the Arts Club.
Worth 4 points

STEVE COOGAN

There's some bar in Hove where all the comedians down here hang out, but I'll be buggered if I can remember the name. I know he has a favourite pub in Hanover but if I told you which one it was he'd probably stop going. Besides, you don't get 20 points that easily.
Worth 20 points

HERBIE FLOWERS

Played with every rock god from Bowie and T-Rex to Lou Reed, and got paid a measly £12 for writing the bassline to 'Walk On The Wild Side'. Probably best loved however for writing the classic pop ballad 'Grandad'. See him down the Komedia doing his double bass thing. If you want a good rock'n'roll story, ask him about the time he was in The Wombles on Top Of The Pops
Worth 10 points

DAVID THOMAS
FROM PERE UBU

Strictly for the music lovers this one. Look for him striding around Hove like some crazy Ignatious Reilly from Confederacy of Dunces. Hmmm I feel I've lost a few of you here, never mind, read on.
Worth 20 points

MARK WILLIAMS
FROM THE FAST SHOW

Found at Kambis grabbing a take-away kebab or hanging around pubs like the Lion and Lobster. Remember the Father Ted episode with Victor Meldrew before you go up to him and say 'Suits you Sir '.
  Worth 15 points.

MARK LITTLE

You'll find him in the Old Lanes making documentaries about vegetarian cafés or hosting the odd event down on the beach. Don't mention Bouncer.
  Worth 10 points

NICK BERRY

The shiny nosed superstar can often be seen walking his 4 Scottie dogs on the beach in the morning. Don't start singing 'Every Loser Wins' as he is known to get aggressive and recently hurled one of his dogs at a journalist from The Argus, just for saying - *'Hello, hello, hello, what's all this then?'*
  Worth 8 points

PATSY ROWLAND

Better known as the frustrated secretary in many of the Carry On movies, whose main role seemed to be pursuing Kenneth Williams around the office desk for a snog and a grope.
Usually seen chasing thin, blond, gay men down St. James's Street in Kemptown...
  Worth 17 points

*I'm sorry I couldn't resist the chopper joke.

If you've been missed out of our spotter's guide and feel that you ought to be included, please write to us finishing the following sentence.

I think I'm famous enough to be in your guide because ....
....
Please enclose £10 and a signed photo. If you are a local celebrity or just have been in The Bill a couple of times this will not be sufficient.

WHERE TO TAKE A GOOD STROLL

The Marina Breakwater

Down near the Marina is a breakwater that extends for about a quarter of a mile out to sea. Take a walk there at sunset and you won't regret it. If you go when the sea is a bit rough it can be wonderfully hairy. It'll take you about 20 minutes to walk there from the pier so try and time it well for sunset. Then you could stick around in the Marina for a drink (bad idea) or walk back into town and flop around at Alleycats (good idea).

Rottingdean

From the Palace Pier head left past the Marina and you'll reach Rottingdean in about one and a half hours. Most of the path from the Marina onwards has been carved out of the imposing, chalky cliffs. This, with the magnificent views of the sea, makes this walk unusual and spectacular at the same time (it's good by bike too). As you get closer to the village you'll start to come across rockpools* and little coves where people go winkle-picking and crab-fishing. Look out for fossils too, I found a Stegosaurus there last year.

*See Good Places To Go, Rockpooling Section

On arrival in Rottingdean, you must have refreshments at Sally's Tip Top Tea Shop, which also doubles as a bizarre junk shop of stuff like Mr T mugs and jigsaws. From here stick around for hot pies and a beer, then get the bus home.

CREATURES OF THE SALTY DEPTHS

Sealife Centre
Marine Parade, opposite the Palace Pier (01273) 604234
Adults £5.50 • Children £3.95

A couple of kippers and a dead dog floating in the shark tank. OK, I'm only kidding, but realistically if you've ever been to one of these places abroad it will probably seem a bit disappointing. Let's face it, with the exception of crabs, fish and toilet paper there's not a lot else in the English Channel these days.

There are a few interesting things inside, and the underwater tunnels are good, but this place does need updating, with better facilities and more interactive features to justify the hype and the expense.

Rockpooling

Past the Marina on the way to Rottingdean there are some fabulous rockpools where you can find edible spider and shore crabs, sea anemonies, little fish and the occasional beached giant squid. If you're in the car, drive to

Rottingdean (just follow the coastal road heading towards Eastbourne), head to the seafront there, past the white pub and turn right. From the Palace Pier it'll take 10 minutes to cycle and 30 minutes to walk.

Dolphin Spotting
Stephen Savage (01273) 424339

There has been an increase in the sightings of dolphins along the coast, in particular Bottlenose dolphins. I must stress that to spot one is rare but the best time to see them is hightide between May and September. Between the two piers and around the Marina are your best viewing spots.

  If you do see one, phone this chap above and make him very happy, he's currently tracking all dolphin and whale activity along the South coast.

Sport

SWIMMING

Saltdean Lido
Saltdean Park Road,
Saltdean (01273) 880616
£2.80 adults • £1.50 children

Original open-air Art-Deco swimming pool, 15 minute drive from Brighton. It looks stunning, has plenty of chairs and tables outside and is worth a visit for those of you who love to swim in style. Open last weekend in May to the end of September.

Pells Pool At Lewes
North Street, Lewes (01273) 472334 Open 12-6pm term Weekend and school holidays 12noon-7.30pm

Open air swimming pool. 'Bit nippy at times. Plenty of space for lounging if you don't mind being surrounded by snogging teenagers.

Prince Regent
Church Street (01273) 685692

Across the road from the Pavilion, this large pool has plenty of space, some good diving boards and a big slide.

  At weekends, splashing around time is between 10am-12.30pm, the rest of the time is for lane swimming. The boards are also in use for most of the day during the weekend and early evenings during the week. It's still best to phone as timetables change quarterly.

Give the life-savers a smile, they always look so bored here. It's never as glamorous as it looks on telly is it?

The Sea

It's free and there's lots of it. A visit to any seaside is not complete without at least getting your feet wet. It's tradition to swim twice around the West Pier before breakfast here, but for newcomers a quick splash around will suffice.

Be careful when the tides are strong, every year someone gets swept away by a surprising freak tide.

WATER QUALITY

The quality of the sea-water varies daily, but the good news is that it is at its highest in summer when the suns UV rays kill off most of the harmful bacterias in the water. If you have any concerns, contact Surfers Against Sewage for a more truthful account of the quality of our coastal waters than the souped-up crap the water authorities tell you.

Tel. 01872 553001
www.scip.org.uk/surfers.

LOCAL SPORTS CENTRES

Stanley Deason
Wilson Avenue (01273) 694281
Only open 5.30pm onwards during the week
All day at weekends

Squash, table tennis, badminton, basketball, volleyball, gym, astro-turf pitches, circuit training, and aerobics.

Portslade Sports Centre
Chalky Road, Portslade
(01273) 411100

Squash, fitness, badminton, snooker.

King Alfred Centre
Kingsway, Hove (01273) 290290

Tropical style pools, badminton, table tennis, martial arts classes, gymnasium. Crêche available, phone for details.

Bowline Bowling Ltd
Below the King Alfred Leisure Centre, King Alfred Tenpin Lanes, Kingsway (01273) 290300
Cheapest game is Mon-Fri 10am-2pm only £1.10 per person and 70p-shoe hire. Open Mon-Sat 10am-11pm, Sun 10am-6pm

Moulsecoomb Leisure Centre
Moulsecoomb Way (01273) 622266

Badminton, table tennis, squash, basketball, roller-skating, gymnasium, sauna and aerobics.

Pulse Station
23-25 Kings Road Arches

Solomon semi-soft boot skates for hire. £3.50 per hr. £50 deposit required or a passport.
Open 10.30am until no one wants any more boots. Open June-Sept.

WATERSPORTS

Sunhire Watersports Rental
185 Kings Road Arches
(01273) 323160

Open May to September and found under the promenade between the two piers. Choose from windsurfing, canoeing or hiring a catamaran or sailing dinghy. They also do water-skiing, which includes tuition, but at £72 per hour you'd have to really like water-skiing or be stinking rich. I know which I'd prefer.

Hove Lagoon
Western End of Hove promenade
(01273) 424842

Windsurfing, sailing, canoeing and they do a special 2-hour taster session for adults and kids at £15 and £20 a shot respectively.

Weird Things To Do

THE GREAT OUTDOORS

Country And Western Weekend
For info (01273) 701152

Spend a weekend on a ranch in Horsham where you'll meet Red Indians in tepees, gamblers, cowgirls and cowboys. You can also expect rodeo, live bands, fishing and err… owls.

Why spend your time in a sweaty club drinking your money away when you could wear a racoon on your head and be a Wild West hero? Contact Colin on the number above for more details.

Llama Trekking
For info (01273) 835656
Running Weds and Sat April-Oct
Llama for one £30. Share a Llama with a friend?
(Ooh, suits you sir!) £45

Just you, the rolling hills, the sun beating down…and your trusty llama by your side. From April to October take a 5-mile ramble over the Downs, a packed lunch is included and will be carried by your llama. It is expensive but when would you ever get the opportunity again?

I know my imagination gets the better of me sometimes, but this is for real. Truth is often stranger than fiction.

Adventures Unlimited
64 Edward Street (01273) 681058
adventure.unlimited@virgin.net

I once spent a brilliant Saturday with a load of friends playing British bulldogs, hide and seek, lateral thinking games and clambering over assault courses thanks to these guys. Not only was it fun and fairly cheap, but we were also entertained by some shameless flirting between my friend Stilly and the organiser.

Needless to say, I thoroughly recommend them, and you should know that they also do loads of other outdoor pursuit days like canoeing, climbing and abseiling.

The events all take place outside Brighton but they do provide free transport if you need it. Book well in advance for summer events.

Adventure Activities With Keith Fleming

Blackland Farm Mid Sussex
01444 235258

No relation to Bob, he won't be coughing all over you. Expect a full packed day or weekend that could include rock climbing, canoeing, orienteering, high ropes, mountain biking, abseiling, archery, and the best zip wire I've ever been on.

The farm is set in the middle of really beautiful woodland and is the perfect setting for your weekend adventures. For what you get, it's fantastic value. Ah, the great outdoors.

£150 per day for a minimum of 4 people, rising by £35 per extra adult. Tents are all provided for camping but are self-catering.
£280 for a weekend, rising by £30 per extra adult. £5 each extra for bike-hire.

WHERE TO CONTACT THE DEAD

Brighton National Spiritualist Church
Edward Street (opposite Devonshire Pl) (01273) 683088

It all starts off surprisingly similar to Christian services, not least because the hymns are the typical tuneless mumbling affairs, except instead of God, you give praise to 'the greater vibration'. Expect a bit more chat and another hymn, then it all picks up when the guest clairvoyant comes on.

Most of these guys are commanding speakers and come across in an American preacher style. There's a prep talk, some fabulous shaky hands business, then the dead will start to communicate (through him) with a few members of the congregation.

Don't always expect to get chosen, but if you are fortunate enough, they'll ask you to speak, so that the spirits pick up on your vibrations. What follows are nuggets of advice and information for you from the spirit world, which are channelled through his voice, and all done to the accompaniment of the shaky hands. Whether it works without this I don't know.

At some point, someone you once knew will manifest through him and communicate with you.

SÉANCES

If you are serious about wanting to be involved with a séance group you can e-mail the Cheeky Guide with your name and phone number. We will pass it on, and they will explain what is required. Unless you are staying in Brighton for some time though, this will not be possible.

If invited you will be expected to take the evening seriously, but I can guarantee you will have plenty of fun. It's all in the pitch dark and starts with singing stuff like 'Roll Out The Barrel' and 'Daisy, Daisy' to get the energy going. Then, once the spirits have manifested through the medium, watch out for stuff moving around the room and hope that you don't spend the night with a chair on your head as one lady did.

Also expect to get covered in ectoplasm and have some questions ready for when you meet some of the fantastic characters such as James the Victorian transvestite comedian. If you ask, the ghosts will tell you who your spirit guide is. Do I get a Buddhist monk or Native American Indian chief like everyone else? No, I get a chicken called Cyril.

At the end of the night you might not all believe what you have seen, but you should have had an enjoyable experience. And it's something to tell the grandchildren.

The time I was picked, I apparently met my Grandad, whose message was –

'stop worrying about your ears sticking out.'

I don't know what this meant because I never have worried about this, but then he always was a bit of a joker.

Afterwards it's cheese, biscuits and a chat, a flick through Psychic News, and then a well-earned breakfast at the Hand in Hand.

Sunday services are at 11am and 6.30pm.

Brighton And Hove Central Spiritualist Church

Half way down Boundary Passage opposite the Gull and Gherkin on Western Road.
Clairvoyances: Mon 3pm,
Sat 7pm
Healing: Tues 1-3pm

PALMISTS & CLAIRVOYANTS

Margaret

64 Elm Grove (01273) 683623
Open Tues-Sat 10am-3.45pm
Closed 12noon-1pm

When you step in here, be ready to take a timewarp back thirty years or more. The walls are littered with fading newspaper articles and curling black and white photos showing Margaret on old TV shows. You feel like you're in a Rita Tushingham movie and Margaret looks and plays the part magnificently.

The readings take around twenty minutes in a tiny room at the back of the shop where she will read your palm or tell your fortune from a pack of cards. Along with the usual stuff like '*you know someone who reads The Daily Mail*', Margaret also said some pretty accurate and insightful things the last time I visited. The readings range from £11 to £15. Go on, treat yourself to a seaside speciality from a true professional.

Professor Mirza

On the seafront between the piers

There's a quote from Jimmy Greaves outside, which is obviously a mark of quality, but unfortunately the professor didn't want to be in our guide unless we paid him!

Pets get their paws read for free every other Saturday at Margaret's

Paul Hughes-Barlow
295 Kings Road Arches, under the
Palace Pier (01273) 677206
Open Mon-Sun 12noon-6pm

The only palmist in Brighton I met
whose room was full of books
rather than gypsy gear and the
usual mystical paraphernalia.
Friendly and honest about his
profession and with a good
knowledge of the occult sciences,
I warmed to him and his
reassuringly boyish laugh. Probably
a good choice if you're looking
for something beyond the usual
seaside nonsense. First sittings are
a standard £15.

STUFF THAT LEGENDS ARE MADE OF

Coopers For Haircuts
27 Baker Street

Probably the cheapest barber's in
the country. The window is
adorned with brown peeling
photos of gentlemen from the
60s, sad plastic heads with
lopsided wigs stare at you
miserably and a sign declaring
'Haircuts 120p' is written in pencil
and stuck in the window.

Mr Cooper is believed to
have been Montgomery's
personal hairdresser during the
war and even have cut
Eisenhower's hair on the odd
occasion. Legend has it that he
only does crew cuts and once

chased someone down the street
for asking for a 'Mick Jagger'.

Although he's a lot frailer, now
he'll still get annoyed if he catches
you loitering outside his shop so
be discrete if taking photos.
Whether or not you want to risk
having your lovely locks chopped
here is your gamble, but my
friend Oz once took the plunge
and was perfectly happy with the
results.

I'm sure Mr Cooper must get
fed up with people taking the
mickey, so have a bit of respect. It
is funny though.

Tony Young Autographs
138 Edward Street (01273)732418
Opening times seem to be akin to
MajorMajorMajorMajor's office
in Catch 22.
In theory....Mon-Fri 10am-
12noon and 1-3pm
Sat 10am-12.30 pm

Twinned with Coopers, this
tumble down shop rescued from
the 1950s has a surreal and
curling collection of autographed

photos and bizarre oddities.
Where else could you get a copy
of the homicide report of the JFK
assassination and a broken banjo?

Worth a visit for fans of The
Twilight Zone but treat him with
respect, he's an old man and
dislikes rowdy people in the shop.

D & K Rosen Clothiers
Top of Church Street
Open Mon-Sat 10am-5.30pm

You don't have a look around here,
you have an adventure. The owner is
one of Brighton's most eccentric
characters, well-known for his bizarre
banter, and the shop is a Twilight
Zone of second hand suits, fez and
other gentleman's attire.

*Rumour has it that this is the
place that inspired the 'Suits You'
sketch from The Fast Show. Legends
don't come much better than this.*

HAVE A SURREAL AFTERNOON IN BRIGHTON

Put on your silliest hat, pack up some sandwiches and head off to Baker Street for your first destination, a compulsory crew-cut at Coopers for 120p. The less adventurous among you may simply want to enjoy the window display.

From here, head past the Level to the Lewes Road and take a first right at the big traffic lights. Number 64 Elm Grove is your next port of call, where you will need to part with £15 to discover what the future holds from mystic Margaret.

Try not to be frightened by her make-up and listen carefully to what nuggets of wisdom she imparts to you.

At the very top of Elm Grove have a quick cuppa at Beckie's café where you can buy fake designer perfume or maybe just fondle the gnomes.

From here cross over and follow Tenantry Down Road for a stunning view as you pass through Brighton's shanty town. The curve of houses you can see in front of you is Roundhill Crescent where Genesis P. Orridge used to live. The strange little huts on either side of you are occupied by Brighton's flourishing Amish community. Keep your walkmans well hidden at this point or you may have a bloodbath on your hands. At the end of the road take a left and look for the entrance to Woodvale Crematorium.

This vast graveyard is remote and enchanting, and should make you feel like you've left Brighton behind. Have a look for Crowley's remains or just relax and enjoy the scenery.

Leave by the main exit at the bottom, and now start heading into town. On your way back, visit the Country and Western shop on Lewes Road, and buy yourself a CD from the strange music stall in the Phoenix Gallery. To round off your afternoon, find the Basketmakers Pub, tucked away at the bottom of the North Laines. Search the tins on the wall to see who can find the strangest message inside, and then leave one of your own. The best messages that I find will appear in next year's guide.

Mind Body Spirit

FROM YOGA AND TAI CHI *classes to Buddhist centres and homoeopaths, Brighton has them all and in abundance. This is a town rich in self-development and soul-searching where in the corner of every park you'll find someone meditating, or at lest reading about it. If you're curious about what day courses are on offer or if you need somewhere to meditate or practice yoga, your best starting point is to pick up a copy of New Insight from the shops in the Lanes.*

I have developed many new interests from yoga to Ayurveda thanks to living in a town where anything goes and where so many different lifestyles co-exist together. Sure there's the usual mystical crap, like places where your stick insect can have its aura cleansed, but if people believe in it, what's the harm? I love the fact that Brighton people on the whole are tolerant and open-minded. After

all, why shouldn't you be able to enjoy meditating as well as clubbing? And where else could you indulge your wildest New Age fantasy and learn to sing like Tom Jones whilst having your bottom cleaned in our new Welsh Colonic Irrigation Centre?

YOGA AND MEDITATION

The Buddhist Centre

14 Tichborne St (01273) 772090
Open 1-3pm weekdays for visitors
Drop-in meditations
Wednesday 1-2pm and
7.30-9.30pm (donation)
Drop-in yoga
Tues 6-7.15pm, Thurs 5.45-7.15pm,
Fri 12.45- 2pm (£3.50/£3)

The group are part of The Friends Of The Western Buddhist Order and their new centre is situated just off the beaten track in the North Laines. It has two stunning meditation and yoga rooms and a library where you can drop in to study or borrow books and tapes for a nominal fee. Look out for more unusual stuff going on here too, like theatre and lectures. I went to a great talk in May where a Buddhist theatre director talked about the genius of Tommy Cooper and Frankie Howerd. Sunday school was never like this.

The Brighton Natural Health Centre

27 Regent Street (01273) 600010

Parallel to Gardner Street, this centre does a wide range of drop in classes, in particular different styles of dance ranging from Jazz and Salsa to contemporary. Along with this comes yoga with a variety of different tutors including the very lovely Peter Blackaby.

Phone or drop in for details of times.

Natural Bodies

(The Green Door) Jew Street, behind Bond Street (01273) 677949
They also do massages, shiatsu, chi kung, feldenkrais…
Classes take place lunchtimes and most evenings. Phone to check or look in New Insight for details

This place does about 10 yoga classes a week, all of them drop-in and at different times of the day. It's a bit of a labyrinth inside the building (it's full of strange voodoo heads and other weird stuff), but follow the screams and you'll find the class on the first floor.

I can personally recommend them as I've been going for about two or three years now and my mum doesn't tell me off for slouching any more. The teachers are friendly and the classes are only 3 to 4 quid for one and a half hours.

Evolution Arts And Natural Health Centre

2 Sillwood Terrace (off Western Road) (01273) 729803

Weekly Iyengar yoga drop-in classes run Tuesday to Saturday at various times. They also do a wide range of one-off workshops from creative writing to mosaics and dramatherapy.

ASTROLOGICAL CHARTS

Both of these gentlemen are experienced Astrologers and all-round good eggs. For a sitting you will just be required to know the exact time and place of your birth. (Ask your mum if you can't remember).

Pete Watson

(01273) 699203
brightpete@yahoo.com

Consultant astrologer and lecturer at the Urania Trust and the Astrological Lodge of London. Personal chart readings as an aid to enhancing self-awareness and personal development.

Tim Burness
35 Guildford Street (01273) 271469

All readings taped, with personal interpretation. I asked Tim which famous people he'd worked with. He reeled off a few well-known names which included Chesney Hawkes, and then begged me not to mention this to you. Mum's the word.

FLOATATION TANKS

The Crescent Clinic
37 Vernon Terrace (01273) 202221
Open 9-5pm Mon-Fri
£20 per session

Located just by the Seven Dials roundabout. Initial sessions last one and a half hours, and include an introduction from trained members of staff.

SHOPPING

Neil's Yard
Kensington Gardens

Comprehensive stock of herbs, essential oils, homoeopathic remedies, vitamins and self-help books. If you're after a free consultation, a Chinese herbalist drops in every Thursday between 3 and 5pm, and a nutritionalist comes Fridays 12.30-2.30pm. The staff will also give advice on common illnesses and can recommend practitioners for anything more serious. The most usual complaints they deal with are stuff like colds and hay fever, but recently some guy came in for herbal hormone replacements for his dog. Typical Brighton.

Lotus Emporium
Gloucester Street (01273) 674742
Open Tue-Sat 11am-6pm
Sun 12-5pm • Mon 12noon-6pm

A whole variety of excellent oils/soaps and resins are sold here for aromatherapy enthusiasts. The soaps look so good that the customers have taken to eating the samples. Try and avoid this if you want to look cool. If you can't place the accent, the friendly girl working here is French-Australian.

Winfalcon's Holistic Shop And Healing Centre
28 Ship Street (01273) 728997
Open Mon-Sat 10(ish)-5.30pm
Sun 12noon-4pm

The usual New Age assortment of crystals, tarots, books and videos that wouldn't look out of place in Glastonbury. Pop in and have your aura photographed…

WHERE TO FIND OUT MORE

The Alternative Practitioners Directory
This is a comprehensive list of all local practitioners who do everything from acupuncture to past-life regression. It's only 40p and you'll find it in places like Neil's yard.

NEW INSIGHT

www.brighton.co.uk/New-Insight
(01273) 245956 e-mail:
New-Insight@brighton.co.uk

Monthly alternative lifestyle
magazine with well-written articles
and a comprehensive diary of
workshops, events and regular
classes around Brighton. A must
for any visitor looking for a
weekend that doesn't just revolve
around pubs and clubs.

Shopping

BRIGHTON *can be a shopaholics paradise, especially if you're a lover of antiques, fashion, jewellery, music, kitsch and all things retro. The most colourful areas with the best shops are definitely the North Laines and the Old Lanes. For the less adventurous, Western Road and the Churchill Square Shopping Centre have everything that you'd expect to find in a high street.*

The North Laines area is particularly good, not only for its cool selection of clothes and records but also for the more unique shops like the Mexican themed Revolución or the saucy but stylish Pussy. Get into the mood here and you'll find yourself going home with a wrestling mask, a Mod suit, a tie dye candle and a pair of fetish shoes. And you only popped out for a loaf of bread.

The Old Lanes are more renowned for jewellery and antiques but there's also a fair selection of clothes shops; some good, others just expensive crap. Think of it this way, if the North Laines were Eric Morcambe, the Old Lanes would be Ernie Wise.

Before you rush off with your credit cards; don't get up too early! Shops here can open notoriously late (especially in the North Laines) and not always at the same time every morning. So do yourself a favour, have a long night out and get up at the same time as nearly everyone else here: around 11am.

RECORD SHOPS

Unless your idea of a good record shop is Woolworths, you owe it to yourself to buy a few ultra cool and unusual records while you're here. For a town of its size, the choice is superb and many friends' bank accounts have come a cropper whilst visiting. How could you resist that old Howard Jones 12inch on original clear vinyl? The North Laines is a good starting point for second hand and unusual records.

Audio Lounge

32 Trafalgar Street 01403 570635
Open Mon 12noon-5.30pm
Tues-Sat 10.30am-5.30pm

Vinyl-only specialists of underground house, techno and breakbeats. The shop is done out like a mini bar and you are more than welcome to hang out, smoke a fag and listen to the latest tunes. They'll even make you a cup of tea if you ask nicely.

Borderline

41 Gardener Street
Open Mon-Sat 10am-5.30pm
Sun 12noon-4pm

This colourful place has consistently stocked an amazing range of music ever since I moved here in the 30s. The shop is small, but avoiding chart music and the obvious means they have an incredible selection of re-issued Jazz, Soul, Psychedelia, Exotica and Soundtrack, mixed with modern Electronica and Indie. Most is on CD but there is a smaller selection on vinyl. If you can find a bad record here I'll change my name to Barbara.

CD, Record And Video Classics

28a Tidy Street (01273) 694229
Open Tues-Sat 10.15am-5.30pm
Closed Mon and Sun

You'll find a meaty selection of classical music on vinyl and CD here, together with an assortment of second hand videos. Lovers of the more exotic might find some Stockhausen and Varesse albums if really lucky. Most of the videos are fairly typical stuff but they often have a good selection of sci-fi like Dr Who, The Prisoner and Star Trek.

Different Music

12 Brighton Square (Old Lanes)
(01273) 202695 Open Mon-Sat
10am-6pm Sun 12noon-5pm

I buy a lot of CDs here because all the stock is new, varied and most of it under £7. Great selection of Jazz, Soundtrack and Easy Listening together with all your pop favourites from the 60s to present day.

Edgeworld

Above Hive, half-way down
Kensington Gardens
Open Mon-Sat 10.30am-6pm

Easy to miss, which would be a real shame, especially for hunters of obscure and underground vinyl. The shop specialises in Low-fi, mellow-Country, post-Rock, non-Dance-Electronica and Ska-Punk

stuff ranging from the very heavy to the very silly. Definitely one for The Wire readers. If that's not enough, most of the stuff is under £10 and you can listen to as much as you want before you purchase. Dress code- Goatie beards optional, record bag essential.

The Record Album
8 Terminus Road (01273) 323853
Open Mon-Sat 11am-5pm

Tucked away up the hill, just round the corner from Brighton Station, this is the oldest record shop in the country and is a must for vinyl junkies.

The shop specialises in all types of deleted recordings and rare one-offs, especially soundtrack albums, most of which are new or in excellent condition. Don't expect to find a bargain, prices start around £10 and go up to £75

among others. Plus it's a good place to find out where some of the more low-key gigs are happening too. Don't be afraid to ask for a listen before you buy, the staff are refreshingly unpretentious. They'll happily stock your own CDs as well if packaged properly. Mine's been there for years…

Happy Vibes Recordings
52 Gardener Street (01273) 699904
Open Mon-Sat 10am-5.30pm

Specialists in HipHop and Drum 'n' Bass. It's all on vinyl (naturally) and you can find out where the best dance nights are in town.

Little Gems
Phoenix Gallery 10-14 Waterloo Place Open every Friday and Saturday 11am-6pm (Possibly Wed/Thurs but it varies)

This is a stall set up in the Phoenix Gallery and run by two music lovers whose ad simply reads – 'Records and CDs that are rather strange'. It is indeed a very eclectic and modest selection of (mainly) instrumental

Records & CDs
☆ that are rather ☆
STRANGE
are being sold at the
PHOENIX GALLERY
EVERY FRIDAY & SAT !!!
BY
11 am   6 pm
LITTLE GEMS
10-14 WATERLOO PLACE BRIGHTON BN22NB

or more for that ultra-rare electronic 50s sci-fi B-movie soundtrack. Owner George also supplies records to the BBC, theatre and radio and has an extensive mail order service. When asked recently by Mojo magazine why he doesn't stock CDs, George just shuddered and said – '*uh, those ghastly little frisbees*'.

Recordland
40 Trafalgar Street
(01273) 672512
Open Mon-Sat 10am-5pm

This place has been here for nearly 20 years and stocks an impressive range of CD and vinyl from the 50s to 70s. They specialise in Jazz, Big Band, Easy Listening and Soundtracks.

They are a friendly bunch and owner Geoff was once nice enough to play me a whole selection of jazz records one afternoon when I couldn't decide what I wanted.

Don't forget to have a look upstairs too, there's a good selection of old comedy records, from Woody Allen to Bernard Cribbins, tucked away somewhere.

Rounder Records
19 Brighton Square
(01273) 325440
Open Mon-Sat 9.30am-6pm
Sunday 10.30am-6pm

Stockists of a handsome collection of vinyl for the DJ market as well as plenty of chart CDs. More importantly, the major ticket outlet, for everything from Elvis at the Brighton Centre, to big club nights and other gigs around town and up at the Big Smoke. Dave there assures me he is Brighton's Reggae and alternative Country expert while other talented staff from the past have included Norman Cook and Damien Harris. Those with a keen eye might recognise the shop from a Phats and Small video

Wax Factor
Trafalgar Street (01273) 673744
e-mail al@wax-factor.demon.co.uk
Open Mon-Fri 10am-5.30pm
Sat 9.30am-5.30pm

Sensational collection of second-hand CDs and vinyl and a meaty stock of cult and music literature.
(See Bookshop reviews for more detail)

Bookshops

BIG GUYS

Borders

Churchill Square Shopping Centre,
Western Road (01273) 731122

Big American bookstore chain
which also stocks records. The
Transatlantic slant means that in
the record section I keep coming
across weird stuff like Pat
Benatar, Asia and Uriah Heep. I
just didn't realise there was a
market for this stuff in England.
Maybe *I'm* the one who's out of
touch. They also have the biggest
selection of magazines anywhere
in Brighton. I get my copy of
'Shiver Me Timbers' from here,
the UK's only official magazine for
pirates. Look out for small music
performances and occasional
readings in the café.

Waterstones

55-56 North Street (01273) 327867
and 71-74 North Street
(01273) 206017

The greedy beggars have two
stores on North Street, both of
which deserve a visit. The staff

Urban Records

24 Gardner Street
(01273) 620567
Open 10am-6pm

House, Garage, rare-groove, Funk,
Jazz and more. Two decades of
dance music on new and used vinyl.

Wizard

48 Baker Street
Open Mon-Sat 9.30am-6pm

Worth a look in but only if
you're in the area. Run by a
friendly hippie couple, stock is
limited but cheap. I once saw
loads of different Sonic Youth
CDs in here for £7 each, so you
can get the odd bargain. Why
didn't I buy them? I spent all my
money on Scott 1 to 4 instead,
much to my girlfriend's horror.
They'll also buy all your
unwanted Fatboyslim and
Catatonia for a fair price if it's in
good nick.

are super friendly and seem to have their finger on the pulse of what Brighton readers are looking for. Particularly good stockists of cult and art books and also prone to the occasional visits by the likes of Will Self and other literary luminaries.

LITTLE GUYS

124 Queen's Road
124 Queens Road
(01273) 323105
Open Mon-Sat 10am-5pm

This place doesn't seem to have a name and if you visit you'll see why.

The window display defies explanation and the whole shop looks as if the owner got a huge truck full of books and just emptied them into the shop and said – 'OK, we're open.'

In fact he always reminds me of Michael Caine in 'Educating Rita', after he's had a few. But ask for any title and if he's got it, he'll rummage through a pile and somehow find it. Deserves a visit just to witness this.

Practical Books
14/14a Western Road
(01273) 734602

Specialising in foreign language books ranging from Arabic to Lithuanian with an impressive selection of literature in countless languages too. They also sell quite a lot of personal development and guitar music.

Rainbow Books

28 Trafalgar Street (01273) 605101
Open Mon-Sat 10.30am-6pm
(except Thursdays which are until
7pm for some reason)

There is a good range of cheap
and cheerful second-hand books
here. If you're not sure what
books you want just buy a cup of
coffee, sit down by the window
and browse through a few of
them. Alternatively, sink yourself
into the sofa downstairs and
thumb through the thousands of
30p bargains.

Everything is cheap and the
books are colour-coded for the
different prices. There's also a
selection of old sheet music in
the basement if you're interested.

Sancho Panza

2 Surrey Street (01273) 773054
Open Mon-Sat 11am-6pm
Closed Tuesdays except term
time when you'll catch him at the
Sussex Uni market

Head to Brighton Station, turn left
at the top into Surrey Street and
you'll find this place at the end,
opposite The Evening Star. The
best stuff is usually in the window,
ranging from cheap videos and
spoken word tapes to a whole
mass of books. The choice of
stock is impressive; if you're
looking for cult classics and
underground stuff I guarantee
you'll walk out with some goodies.

If you're a fan of 50s and 60s
American literature, you should
get a copy of the Richard
Brautigan tape here, which
features the ultra-rare album the
author did for Apple records and
also a great documentary.

Tall Storeys Bookshop

88 St. James's Street (01273)
697381 Open Mon-Sat 10am-5.30pm
Sun 2-5.30pm

Five floors of second-hand books
and specialising in art and cinema.
Narrow staircases and intriguing
cubby holes make it a pleasure to
look around. But be careful of the
stairs, last time I was here I fell
down them and felt a real plonker.
So don't expect to see me in there
until the beard has fully grown.

The Little Bookshop
17 Montpelier Place

Owned for the last 26 years by an old couple straight out of the Fast Show and Enid Blyton. It's the usual collection of second hand stuff but if you're not looking for anything too specialised in literature you'll find their stock adequate and exceedingly cheap. Worth a look in if you're in the area, just to see how nice old people can be.

Wax Factor
Trafalgar Street (01273) 673744
e-mail al@wax-factor.demon.co.uk
Open Mon-Fri 10am-5.30pm
Sat 9.30am-5.30pm

If second hand books on the occult, drugs, philosophy, science fiction, Eastern religion and music are your style then this is the place for you. The window display should be enough to pull you in as you drool over all the Crowley, Philip K Dick and Burroughs books. They have a pretty good selection of literature here too, which is just on your right as you walk in. If that's not enough, they also stock one of the best collections of second hand CDs and vinyl in Brighton at reasonable prices. The basement stocks a meaty selection of 7inches and CD singles too. Be prepared for a good half an hour in this place.

COMICS

David's Comic Shop
5 Sydney Street (01273) 691012
Open Mon-Fri 9.30am-5.45pm
Sat 9am-6pm

Independent comics, graphic novels, Star Wars and Buffy The Vampire Slayer related stuff. The staff are friendly, even towards a bumbling novice like me.

Reservoir Frogs (in Hive)
6 Kensington Gardens
(01273) 687802
Open Mon-Sat 11am-6pm
Sun 11am-5.30pm

Two floors of comics, Star Wars figures, gothic gizmos and records (see review of Edgeworld Records in music section). Noisy, busy and definitely worth a browse around. They also stock some unusual magazines, including quite a good selection of fetish, tattoo, grafitti and drug related stuff. Something for all the family.

COOL THINGS FOR THE HOME

Anatolia

98 Gloucester Road
Open Mon-Sat 10.30am-5.30pm

Specialists in all things Turkish, from earthenware to rugs. Check out the Mosque alarm clocks that will wake you every morning with prayers. A modern day kitsch classic.

Euro Deco

36 Gloucester Road
(01273) 687132 Open Mon-Sat 12noon-6pm Sunday 1-3pm

Beautiful but expensive items from the 50s to 70s. Best sellers here are the old French telephones which go for around £50 to £110. Expect a lot of chrome items, groovy lamps, radios and chairs. Deck out your home to look like a set from The Avengers. If you're a collector you should find the odd bargain.

Pussy

Kensington Gardens
Open 10(ish)-5.30pm
Summer Sun 12noon-4.30pm

This very stylish and saucy shop has a wonderfully strange selection of chic and erotic books, fetish china, jewellery, cool furniture and oddities. Definitely one of my favourite shops in Brighton, not least for the nun finger puppets and the nose pencil sharpeners. Think Barbarella meets Frank Lloyd Wright at an Esquivel concert.

Pyramid

9a Kensington Gardens
(01273) 607791 Open Mon-Fri 10am-5.30pm Sun 11am-5.30pm

From exotic toilet seats to Simpsons chess sets and furry lamps. They also do a nice line in chrome fans and lava lamps.

Rin*Tin*Tin

34 North Road
(01273) 6732424
Open Mon-Sat 11am-5.30pm

Interesting collection of pre-70s memorabilia, ranging from magazines, toys, games, radios and posters. You know that petrol globe bedside light you've always wanted, well bugger me if they don't have them here.

MUSICAL INSTRUMENTS

Adaptatrap

26 Trafalgar Street (01273) 672722
Open Mon-Sat 10am-6pm

A cut above the usual collection of ethnic instruments, this place sells a whole range of drums, koras, xylophones, singing bowls, old gongs and horns and many other exotic and strange instruments from all over the world. What's more is that they don't mind you coming in and playing with them. Owner Les is helpful and will smoke an entire roll-up without taking it out of his mouth whilst giving you advice on what to do if you've damaged your congas (ooh missus). The shop is littered with ads for music lessons and if you're sticking around Brighton and need to find that all-essential sitar teacher, this is the place to look. You'll also find out about workshops and gigs here, ranging from Zither recitals to Shamanic drumming weekends.

The Guitar, Amp And Keyboard Centre

79-80 North Road (01273) 676835
Open Mon-Sat 9.30am-5.30pm
Sun 11am-4pm

One of Brighton's great success stories, owner Gary came here years ago with a broken banjo and the gift of the gab. Seven years down the line and the shop has a most impressive stock of acoustic and electronic equipment. These guys have done me some terrific deals in the past and more importantly also proved that music shops do not have to be run by metal morons who are more interested in their own talents than actually selling you a guitar. Best to come early if you want to try out the instruments as it gets awfully packed in the afternoon.

What is it with accordion players anyways ?

Music Exchange

Trafalgar Street (01273) 239356
Open Mon-Sat 10ish-5.30pm

Cheap and cheerful selection of second hand guitars, amps and effects.

If you can stand the smell of stale beer, these guys will burp their way through a friendly haggle.

Software Warehouse
112 London Road (01273) 671290
www.software-warehouse.co.uk
Open Mon-Sat 9am-5.30pm
Closed Sun

I just mention this place because it sells the cheapest recordable CDs in town at 88p each. I've used them and the quality seems fine. Best to phone first though, to check if they have any in, they usually sell out within the first few hours of delivery.

Mamba
96 St. James's Street (01273) 600160
Open Mon-Sat 10.30am-6pm

Lots of second-hand equipment and a friendly haggle with owner Terry.

A good place for someone who's starting into music and doesn't want to spend much. There are some cheap drums in the basement too but they do get snapped up fairly quickly.

Don't forget to ask Terry about his rock 'n' roll days drumming with Van Morrison.

CLOTHES SHOPS

From safari suits for him to rubber catsuits for her, Brighton boasts a meaty collection of retro, exotic and club-fashion clothes shops. Most are located in the North Laines so if you want to get kitted out in something especially slinky for a club night or just want something new for the wardrobe, here's where to go.

Glitzy Tartz
26 Sydney Street (01273) 674477
www.glitzytartz.com
Open Mon-Sat 10am-6pm

Exotic clubwear for girls and adventurous boys, including quality but pricey rubberwear. It's well worth taking a look at these flamboyant and colourful designs and the window display makes Topshop look like Hastings in February.

Inside Glitzy Tartz

Jump The Gun
36 Gardner Street (01273) 626555
Open Mon-Sat 10am-6pm

Very chic and authentic mod wear. Not exactly cheap but Weller drops by every now and again, so I guess it has the stamp of approval.

From the usual Ben Sherman and parkas to their own (more interesting) shirts and a wide and cool range of suits.

Klub Kit
76 North Road (01273) 688144
Open Mon-Sat 10am-6pm

UV body jewellery, glow-in-the-dark ear rings, fluorescent clothes, clubwear and fetish wear for girls. I particularly like their perspex bikinis (but they didn't have my size). Very popular with the exotic club crowd, especially for Endorphine Visions and Wild Fruit.

Mambo
37 West Street (01273) 323505
Open Mon-Sat 10am-6pm
Sun 12noon-6pm

Skateboarding fashion with a range of outrageous Hawaiian style shirts.

Route One
Bond Street (01273) 323633

The guys in here are pretty cool, sell mainly shoes and clothes, but have a decent selection of boards, wheels, trucks etc, and always seem to have some sort of good skate video on the box. They are also pretty knowledgeable on what the current scene is like, so they'll tell you some of the better places to skate if asked nicely.

Yamama
92 Trafalgar Street (01273) 689931
Open Mon-Sat 11am-6pm

Colourful range of interesting and fair priced clothing. They sell great baggy trousers and I really wanted one of their urban t-shirts (but they're women only sizes) so my girlfriend bought one just to annoy me. If the clothes don't appeal, why not try crocheted slippers or that essential travel backgammon set for those long winter evenings in Tibet or when you're next stuck in a Welsh service station?

Ghita Schuy
17 Street George's Road
(01273) 885275 Open Mon-Fri
12noon-5pm Sat 12noon-6pm

Hand made shoes, made to order.

X To Z
Western Road Open Mon-Sat
10am-6pm Sun 11.30am-5.30pm

A rather wild collection of boots and shoes adorns this shop, even if it does feel a bit 80s goth at times. Expect anything from thigh-high boots to glittery DMs. They also do a rather odd collection of faded punk and metal bands T-shirts. Where else could you still buy an Exploited T-shirt?

SECOND HAND CLOTHES

Circe's Island
22 Trafalgar Street

Decorated with plastic birds, palm trees and fishing netting hanging from the ceiling, this place sells second hand quality clothes, shoes and err…fireplaces. Most of the stuff is for women, and my girlfriend says they have a good selection of coats. They've been two fake furs less since she last went in. Be prepared for Mr Miserable who sometimes works here. Opening times – 'When we feel like it.' – Tell him to cheer up.

Cutie
Kensington Gardens Open Mon-Sat 10.30am-5.30pm Sun 12noon-5pm

Interesting collection of second hand clothes and not your usual American 70s gear either. More for the girls this one and check out the bargain basement – everything £3.

Cushy B
56 Sillwood Street (01273) 774888 Open Tues-Sat 12noon-6pm

Fabulous collection of vintage and period women's clothes from Victorian nightwear and sexy slips to dresses, gowns and accessories.

Expect friendly advice on personal grooming (!) from owner Katy, and a nice hot cuppa if you ask nicely.

Rokit
Kensington Gardens (01273) 672053 Open Mon-Sat 9.30am-6pm

Well established and good quality selection of second hand gear, especially for their own range of jeans, Hawaiian and Cuban shirts, flares and track wear. The shop looks really cool and the staff dress to impress.

Starfish
25 Gardner Street (01273) 680868 Open Mon-Fri 10.30am-6pm Sat 10am-6pm Sun 11.30am-4.30pm

Quality retro gear and a foxy owner.

To Be Worn Again
51 Providence Place (01273) 277686 Open Mon-Sat 11am-7pm Sun 12noon-4pm

Tucked away just off Trafalgar Street opposite St. Bartholomews church, this is the biggest second-hand clothing warehouse in Brighton. The choice of stuff is the usual 70s shirts, leather and suede jackets and paisley dresses but as there's more of everything you're more likely to find something groovy for an evening at the Bubblegum Factory. Don't miss the backroom with a great selection of coats including three quarter and full length fake fur coats.

VIDEOS, FILM & MEMORABILIA

Movie Mania
George Street Open Mon-Sat 10.30am-5.30pm Sun 1-6pm

Original posters, photo stills from films, books, old magazines and two terrapins, Geek and Merlin who live in the middle of the shop.

Enterprise Video
49 London Road (01273) 670052
Open Mon-Sat 9am-6pm

There's some good stuff in here. It's all second-hand videos but some of it is a cut above the usual collections of Brat Pack tosh and cheap thrillers. They have a modest selection of Blaxploitation, horror, cult, etc and some deleted stuff and if you can't find what you're looking for there's also a free finder service. Prices range from £2 to £30 for the rare stuff and half price for exchange. Expect

a purchase if you drop by. I got a copy of 'Freaks' from here for £7.

ODDITIES
ACME ART
41 Gloucester Road
(01273) 601639
Best to phone for opening times as they seem erratic at the best of times

The world would be a duller place if there weren't people like Chris MacDonald around. This retired teacher found happiness making strange sculptures from original wood and metal objects and has been established in Brighton for several years now.

There's something very cartoonish and surreal about his work; it's the kind of art you'd expect to find in Terry Gilliam's house. The sculptures make

perfect unusual birthday presents but don't be surprised if they end up sitting on your mantlepiece instead.

Arkham

Arkham

89 Trafalgar Street (01273) 628440
Mon-Sun 11am-6pm Closed Wed

This place stocks an odd assortment of things such as clothes, jewellery, ornaments, sculptures and books. The shop is littered with gargoyle sculptures, Giger artwork (from the first Alien film), Skin Two books and Klimt postcards. It's kind of interesting even if you don't feel part of their vision. *'Imagine Jules Verne meets cyberpunk.'*

Burchell's

103 Gloucester Road
Open Mon-Sat 9.30am-5pm but phone just to be sure

Wholesalers of religious artefacts and icons. A three foot oak crucifix would set you back £235 for example. Opposite the counter however there's always a couple of boxes on the floor of miscellaneous items that you can haggle for, or if you're lucky they'll give you for free. I found a fantastic wooden wallscroll with very kitschy painting on it and parts of a crib set last time I was in. There's usually a few damaged crucifixes in there too.

If you're into religious imagery or need something to spice up your latest junk sculpture, this is the place to come.

Blackout

53 Kensington Place
Open Mon-Sat 10am-6pm

My friend Kirsty adores this shop whose angle is kind of fashion-folk-art mixed with kitsch religious imagery! They do a great selection of own design T-shirts and have some of the best original style jewellery in town. If you're a goth keep away, they have a policy of selling nothing black here, colour is in. Typical stock includes a Tibetan baby carrier for £28, fluorescent loo brushes, Virgin Mary ashtrays and plastic Hindu Gods. I can tell your curiosity has been pricked.

HIGH STREET STORES

If you're looking for the likes of Miss Selfridges and Warehouse you'll find them up by Churchill Square where many of the high street clothes shops for women are concentrated. East Street, Duke Street and Ship Street in the Old Lanes are also good places to start if you're into shops like Kookai, Jigsaw and Next.

ChoccyWoccyDooDah
27 Middle Street (01273) 329462
Open Tue-Fri 10-6pm Sat 10-5pm

You'll forgive the ludicrous name the second you walk in here and take in that sweet smell of Belgian chocolate. The display area is like a Doctor's waiting room full of the most outrageous, over the top chocolate cakes you've ever seen. I saw a spiky fetish chocolate cake recently and one covered in realistic looking chocolate vegetables including carrots and cabbage (!?). Be prepared to pay up to £3000 for some of the top notch wedding cakes though. If that's out of your budget they do chocolate action men for £10, which are well worth becoming a total fatty for.

The Emporium
71a Western Road (01273) 202897
Open Mon-Sat 10am-6pm

Tea and coffee specialists. You can get over 90 types of tea and 20 flavours of coffee, ranging from Swiss chocolate almond and hazelnut to their alcohol flavoured ones such as amaretto and Irish whisky. The owners are a ridiculously amiable couple and describe themselves as '*an unpaid counselling service for all the old ladies in Hove*'.

If you're lucky you'll bump into regular customer Lesley who retells Jack Benny and Groucho Marx jokes. He once said to me – '*It's not so much the shops that are great here, it's the personalities behind them.*' – I think I'd say the same for some of the customers too.

HEMP CORPORATION
24 Church Street (01273) 208708
www.thehempcorp.demon.co.uk
Open Mon-Sat 9.30am-5.30pm
Open Sunday in Summer

It's hemp everything here from the cool clothes to the paper, pasta, hats, toiletries and oil. Even its charming owner Dave is made entirely of hemp. Most predictable comment from customers is '*got any weed*' followed closely by '*can we smoke it when we've finished with it?*' Worth a visit and if you're peckish there's even free hemp seed on the counter.

Hocus Pocus

38 Gardner Street (01273) 572202
Open Mon-Sat 10-6pm Sun 12-4pm

A particularly odd assortment of stuff here from New Age to drug culture. There's a mixture of new age books and accessories and you can have tarot readings and clairvoyance upstairs.

What is special is their comprehensive stock of drug paraphernalia together with a meaty collection of herbal highs from hallucinogenics to ecstasy substitutes. The shop has a similar feel to Amsterdams's smart shops if ever you've been.

My favourite item here is the chocolate maggots and the most-ridiculous-thing-in-the-shop award goes to the socks with names on. What kind of person who smokes pot and reads books on Buddhism wears socks with their name on? 'Dont laugh' said the owner with embarrassment, 'they are our best sellers'. I think Brighton is starting to get me now.

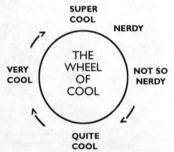

Concept lifted from Eddie Izzard

M&D Hawkins Antique Arms & Armour

27 Meeting House Lane
(01273) 321357
Open Mon-Sat 10am-5.15pm

Souvenir firearms and armour from all periods of history. Get your granny that old Vickers submachine gun she always wanted, or maybe a luger for young cousin Donald. They also have some wild suits of armour and even a helmet from the Iraqi war. Look out for the thank-you message and photo from Ronnie Reagan behind the till. I'll leave it to you to discover the story behind that.

Revolución

31 Sydney Street (01273) 626349
Open Mon-Sat 1.30-6pm

The theme is Mexican. Owner Will is a local celebrity in his own right and if you can drag him away from 'Redneck Rampage' he'll sell you anything from boxing nuns, spicy sauces and voodoo dolls to wrestling masks. 'The masks and wrestling magazines sell particularly well,' says Will, 'there's a lot of perverts in Brighton.'

He can also recommend a good stockist of fancy tequilas, from Mescal to Tarantula.

Taylors (Tobacconist)
19 Bond Street (01273) 606110
Open 9.30am-6pm

A 'THANK YOU FOR SMOKING' sign welcomes you as you enter, and the selection of flavoured tobacco (including chocolate) and Cuban cigars reminds me why it took 10 years to kick such a pleasurable habit. Go on, have a fag.

5,6,7,8 (The Line-Dancing And Country And Western Shop)
40 Lewes Road (01273) 298476
Open Tues-Fri 10am-5.30pm
Sat 10.30am-4.30pm
Closed Sun and Mon

Buy yourself those all important styrrups, boots and stetson and join Brighton's cowboy community. You can also discover about line dancing classes and pick up information on the Country and Western weekends in West Sussex from this wonderfully bizarre shop.

The Pound Shop
North Street near Barclays bank
Open Mon-Sat 9am-5.30pm

A veritable bonanza of bargains. Stock up on food, Xmas presents and condiments. Brighton is not a town of money snobs. Hardly anyone has much of the stuff so we're not too proud to come here. Besides some of the stock is top quality bargain material. If you're a biscuit or chocolate fan like me, go with an empty suitcase…

MARKETS
The Sunday Market
Behind Brighton Station
Open 6am-12pm

As much a part of Brighton as the Pavilion, a weekend here is not complete without the Sunday car-boot. The serious bargain hunters arrive before 7am but if you've had a bender on Saturday night, 11am is a more realistic time to come and you'll still get to see it all. It's the perfect thing for walking up an appetite for late breakfast or early Sunday lunch.

Expect to find record stalls, videos, antiques, clothes, food, weird stuff and loads and loads of crap. One of the strangest stalls is the guy selling manky limbs from Victorian dolls. He's always there, so logic dictates that there must be a regular stream of people who need them. WHO ARE YOU??? Another regular is the CD stall on the far right-hand side which always plays these awful records by 70s Irish comedians. I've yet to see someone walk past, hear it, laugh and then make an impulse buy. Saying that, I've never seen the owner laugh either.

Don't be afraid to haggle. If something seems too expensive, tell them. If they won't take your generous offer of 50p for their Rolf Harris stylophone, take satisfaction in rolling your eyes, huffing, then walk off. If it was a bluff on their behalf they'll run after you and beg forgiveness. At this point, offer 10% less and secure the deal by spitting into your palm and then shaking on it.

To find the market, go into the station, head right and continue until you get to the car-park. Keep walking and it's just behind there.

Saturday
In The North Laines
Upper Gardner Street
Saturdays only 10am-2pm

Nothing to get too excited about, unless your idea of a bargain is a broken cine camera for £30. But you might find a good book or a cheap shirt, and besides, it's pleasant to wander down, and can be a good alternative to being squashed in Kensington Gardens on a hot, busy Saturday afternoon.

Stalls On The Seafront
On Sunday only

If you slept through the alarm at 11am for the station car-boot sale then don't fret. A leisurely stroll between the piers after lunch should help compensate. Here you will find a modest range of stalls selling clothes, books, sunglasses and other stuff. And don't forget to visit the artists quarters nearby, if you haven't already been.

Once at the Sunday market, I found this old tin with a goofy looking vicar sticking out the top. If you turn the handle the head moves up and down. It might have cost 15 quid, but you just don't come across stuff like this every day.

Fruit And Veg Market
Open Mon 7am-1pm Tues-Thurs
7am-5pm Fri-Sat 7am-6pm

Your cheapest option for fresh fruit, veg, fish and other food. There are also plenty of stalls selling things like cut-price tins and dairy products. Perfect for students or if you're doing Brighton on the cheap. Don't buy in bulk though, the stuff here won't last as long as the fruit and veg you buy in Sainsbury's. Do like everyone else, take it home, buy a pizza and watch it rot.

FLEA MARKETS

Snoopers Paradise
7-8 Kensington Gardens
(01273) 602558 Open
Mon-Sat 9.30am-5.15pm

Brighton's largest indoor flea-market. There are two floors of stock and a particularly good collection of unusual 60s clothes, but be prepared to pay through the nose. Don't visit if you have a heart condition – you may find yourself saying things like *'I threw mine away last year and they're selling it here for £200!!!!'* or *'sixty quid for that piece of crap?'*.

"It's a moochers paradise"
Dave from Rounder Records

Kemptown Flea Market
31a Upper St. James's Street
(01273) 624006 Open Mon-Sat
9.30am-5.30pm Sun 10.30am-5pm

Keep going up St. James's Street and you'll find this garish, pink, two-storey building just after the road bends. I somehow prefer it to Snoopers. Sure, there's still a lot of overpriced tat but you can find some really unusual objects and dare I say it – even some bargains? Think Wilf Lunn meets Patrick McNee*.

There isn't much in the way of clothes but there's usually a good stock of cool things for the house,

like 60s lamps. And the Gendarme's hat I bought my mum for Xmas was only a fiver!

(I'd love to know how many of you right now are thinking – 'who the hell are they???')

St. George's Parish Hall
110 Street Georges Road
(opposite the Burlington on Upper
St. James's Street)

The market is every Friday 8am-2pm and simply advertises – *'Fresh eggs and bargains.'* (?!) Make of that what you will.

Auctioneers

Raymond P Inman
Fine Art Auctioneers
35 Temple Street
Mondays only

Make sure not to pick your nose or you may find yourself going home with a Picasso.

The Sunday market down on the sea front

Mullets, Bobs And Mohikans

Headroom

22 Victoria Road (01273) 746964

At £5 a cut, the best value haircut in town for men, and they'll do you everything from a quiff to a skinhead. Recently all but demolished by a runaway car but they still opened for business the next day. True professionals. Best to come before 3pm or you might have a bit of a wait.

Jackson's

9 Manchester Street Open Mon-Fri 9am-5.30pm Sat 9am-3pm

This place is just stunning. Choose your haircut from the countless fabulous cartoons that adorn the wall, from Tony Curtis to Oasis. Not only that, the wall opposite sports 280 bald heads, and outside is a blackboard for thought for the day. Haircuts are cheap and can include a head massage and cup of coffee. No appointments necessary, it's very gay-friendly and women who fancy that barbered look are welcome too.

Classic Cuts

64 Dyke Road (01273) 323495
Open Tue-Thur 9am-5pm
Fri 9am-6pm Sat 9am-4pm

A welcoming unisex hairdressers in the heart of the Seven Dials. Popular with young professionals, trendy students and elderly locals alike.

Friendly owner Kevin will chat to everyone in the same casual manner and don't be surprised if saucy subjects are the topic of the day.

Jacq Aris

Basement of Trade Delegation, 16 Sydney Street (01273) 410317 mobile 0795 7314133
Appointments only.

Stylish chops from the woman in black. And while you're there, tell her to get a move on with her novel.

COSTUME RENTAL

If like me you like to ham it up as Father Christmas and Wonder Woman every now and again, it's good to know where to get those all-essential items for a night out at Vavavavoom! or Wild Fruit.

These are the only two places that I know of.

Masquerade
26 Preston Road
(01273) 673381
Mon-Sat 10am-5.30pm

Stocking the more traditional fancy dress gear, this place has an inexhaustible range of costumes, much more than is just on display.

Expect everything from Vampires to Bart Simpson. Some costumes are much better than others, so try on a few before choosing. And be wary of the latex masks, they might look good on, but are a bit much to have to wear all night.

It's also a good place for picking up novelty facial hair and wigs. I don't know if these things are important to you but I always feel secure in a new town, knowing where I can buy a false moustache.

Revamp
11 Sydney Street (01273) 623288

Going on more for the glam stuff than Masquerade, you can hire anything from thigh-high boots to Las Vegas style Elvis gear. They have a really wide range of exotic 70s wear, especially platforms, and if it's fluffy and feathery you'll find it here.

There are plenty of clothes for sale here too, as well as joke shop gags and other oddities like vibrators and body paint.

Revamp in the North Laines

Food

With over 400 restaurants to choose from, more cafés per square mile than any other town its size and a whole range of exotic food shops, I'll be very annoyed if you end up in McDonalds after all this hard work.

LATE-NIGHT EATING

Grubbs

27 York Place and
89a St. James's Street
(01273) 688111 Open Mon-Wed
12noon-1am Thur 12noon-2am
Fri-Sat 12noon-3am Sun 12pm-12am

They do a wide range of vegetarian and meat burgers, starting at £1.63 for a regular, but why do that when for twenty pence more you can have Barbecue, Malaysian, Tropical or Hawaiian?

You can sample a bit of Brighton nightlife here most evenings if you want to stick around and eat, but I can't say it's particularly pleasant inside. Be prepared for a bit of a wait though, even when it's empty I've waited up to 15 minutes just for one burger. And is it my imagination or do half the staff always seem to be nursing outrageous hangovers? Maybe you should ask them which parties they go to.

The Market Diner

19-21 Circus Street (01273)
608273 Open Mon-Sun 9.30pm-
11am Fri 9.30pm-9am

Found on Circus Street just past the Art block on Grand Parade and one of the most famous landmarks in Brighton's nightlife. This is your typical greasy fry-up café with ashtrays made from the foil base of Mr Kipling apple pies. It is however a must for that post-club hunger and a place to meet and socialise with deranged and dangerous people. Their breakfast gut-buster is near legendary and will satisfy the greediest of pigs, as they certainly don't economise on the lard (although they do a veggie/vegan version, too).

My friend Duncan recommends that you ask for a cup of tea *without* a fag end in it.

The Brighton Bystander
1 Terminus Road (01273) 329364
Open Mon-Sat 8am-12Midnight
Sun 8am-12Midnight

Opposite the station, this greasy spoon café will deliver the goods if your taste buds are non-too discerning. Quite a chilled atmosphere if you get a table, but don't let them rope you into giving a hand behind the till, as I've witnessed here on at least two occasions. Good place for posters and fliers and a perfect opportunity to impress the staff by cracking the joke – *'Waiter, there's a flier in my soup'*.

Also part of the same Brighton's own chain: the (much cleaner) Innocent Bystander, 54 Preston Street (01273) 728131. Where they also do cocktails.

Café Continental
Castle Square (01273) 747085
Open Mon 7.15am-6pm
Tues-Thur 7am-11pm
Fri -Sun 7am(9am Sun)-4am

This café is a nice change from the usual late-night eating places. It's clean, you can get dishes that don't include chips, and all the staff are foreign girls, which, according to the manageress, is one of their best attractions, although the American breakfast with waffles and maple syrup would probably come a close second.

Subway Subs & Salads
146 North Street
(01273) 276551
Mon-Sat 8am-3.45am

Strip-neon lights and Happy Shopper-style baguettes.

Shakies
19 Old Steine
(01273) 620200
Mon-Sun till 3am

The food here is only to be used in hand-to-hand combat.

24 HOUR SUPERMARKETS

B2
Queens Road
(by the station)
Western Road (by Lansdowne Place, Hove)

A far cry from the days of old when you'd pop to the 24-hour garage for a loaf of floppy bread and some rizlas, although they do have the obligatory bags of charcoal by the door.

Expect fairly fresh bread, croissants, a meat counter and even Haagen Daas ice cream. So there is life after Happy Shopper after all.

SPECIALIST FOOD SHOPS

Yum Yum Oriental Market
22-23 Sydney Street (01273) 606777 Open Mon-Sat 10am-6pm Friday open late upstairs Sun 12noon-5.30am

A great selection of oriental food. Along with fresh herbs and vegetables there are some excellent Chinese cooking sauces and utensils. And where else could you get tinned squid and tai chi slippers? (By that I don't mean both in the same tin). See our restaurant guide for their noodle bar upstairs.

The Cheese Shop
17 Kensington Gardens (01273) 601129 Open Mon-Sat 10am-5pm

Always smelling of pongy feet but with a superb selection of the finest cheeses. Look out for 'cheese of the week', some of the best sarnies in town and French cider. I asked the woman behind the counter how many times a day someone walked in and quoted The Monty Python cheese shop sketch to her, and she answered – 'What sketch?'

Deb's Deli
4 Gardner Street (01273) 604925 Open Mon-Sat 9am-5pm

Although most of the tins and food in the window look as if they may well have seen their heyday, don't be taken in by this first impression. The selection here is amazing, ranging from potato lutkas to tinned snails, mushroom ketchup and a wide choice of deli fillings to go on normal bread, rye or bagels. And the cheapest smoked salmon and cream cheese bagel in town.

Appetites Delicatessen
68 Dyke Road (01273) 323266 Opne Mon-Sat 9am-6pm Sun 9am-2pm

Here you can find anything from the best veggie haggis to goats milk yoghurt and a wide range of cheeses, chocolates, unusual sauces and pasta.

The staff are friendly and you're likely to witness some good neighbourhood banter if you pop by in the afternoon.

Italian Shop
91/94 Dyke Road (01273) 326147 Open Mon-Sat 6am-7pm

Mediterranean heaven in the heart of the busy Seven Dials, with one the friendliest shop owners in Brighton. If he starts singing 'O Sole Mio' for you in front of the other people in the shop, just smile

FOOD

Who will buy my lovely bread?

politely and say 'Lei ha delle gambe bellissime', which means 'you have a great voice'. The food is fabulous and if you're planning a picnic, the bread is made in heaven.

The Pasta Shop
12b Meeting House Lane
(01273) 723522 Open Mon-Sat
10am-6pm Sun 12noon-5pm

Proper homemade pasta, and a selection of fresh sauces which they can heat up for you to take away. Go and eat it on the beach and look down upon all those miserable suckers who bought a dehydrated burger from the pier.

Spaghetti Junction
60 Preston Street (01273) 737082
Open Tue-Sat 10am-6pm Mon
10am-5.30pm Thu 10am-7pm

First class fresh pasta (spinach and ricotta ravioli, fettuccine, etc), homemade sauces and ready-made meals to take home. Speciality melts

are their forte. Ciabatta or foccaccia rolls start at £1.50 and fresh pasta is £1.90 per lb.

Ryelight Chinese Supermarket
48 Preston Street (01273) 734954
Open Mon-Sat 11am-6pm
Sun 11am-5pm

Smaller than Yum-Yums but with everything a good Chinese supermarket should stock.

Taj Mahal International Foods
21a/b Bedford Place
(01273) 325027
Open Mon-Sun 9am-8pm

Specialist food retailers of Indian, Middle Eastern, Greek, Chinese, and Malaysian grains and spices.

HEALTH FOOD SHOPS
Infinity Foods Cooperative Ltd
25 North Road (01273) 603563
Open Mon-Sat 9.30am-5.30pm
Fri 9.30am-6pm

Brighton's much loved health food shop stocks everything for your heart's desire. Yogi teas, organic turnips and tofu burgers all under one roof, and bread is baked on the premises. Whether you're a veggie, vegan, or allergic to yak hair, you'll find something delicious here.

their sandwiches are probably the cheapest in town.

If your feet need a rest there's a proper café upstairs. Locally known as 'The Pink Shop'. You'll know why when you get there.

Organic Matters
1 New England Street (01273) 689725 Open Mon-Sat 9am-6pm

Looking like a disused pub with two gold Taj Mahal domes on top, this place stocks everything from organic veg and herbs to logs, furniture and hammocks. Round the back they sell direct off-cuts from oak, elm, beech and cherry which you can buy to make unique things for the home. I'm currently working on a model of the Esher staircase, you couldn't give me a hand could you? At Christmas this is also the place for trees. Verdict? Well worth a nose around.

SANDWICH BARS

Veggie/Vegan Sandwich Shop
92a Trafalgar Street (01273) 623332 Open Mon-Sat 7.30am-5.30pm Closed Sunday

Meat-free sandwiches that aren't cheese and tomato.

Lanes Patisserie
30 Ship Street (01273) 202106 Open Mon-Fri 9.30am-4pm Sun 9.30am-5pm

Good place to grab a quick snack if walking round the Old Lanes, as

Pat's Place
128 Queen's Road (01273) 325278 Open Mon-Fri 8.30am-4pm Sat 11am-5pm

Big portions and good quality are at the order of the day in this tiny shop. The place is carnivore friendly and if it flies, jumps, ruminates or swims you'll find it here in some form or other. Try their lovely curried panda baguette.

NORTH LAINES CAFÉS

Café Motu
6 Trafalgar Street (01273) 270895 Open Mon-Sat 9am-6pm

Small, chilled-out café in the North Laines which is well-loved for its speciality soups. The spicy ones are particularly good and they all come in enormous bowls which make them pretty good value for money. Very popular for fried breakfasts too.

Dumb Waiter
28 Sydney Street (01273) 270895 Open Mon-Sat 9am-5pm Sun 10am-3.30pm

Fairly cheap café in the North Laines, with a pleasant atmosphere and a few seats outside. Reputedly one of the best veggie breakfasts in town, since the eggs they use come from stray hens they've rescued*. Check the backyard if you don't believe me.

*See the review of Lewes fireworks.

Infinity Café
Gardner Street
Open Mon-Sat 9.30am-5pm

Stylish veggie/vegan café, born out of Infinity Foods' incredible success and with the food to match. Expect queuing at lunchtime, though you should always be able to find a seat upstairs.

OLD LANES CAFES

Coffee Chaos
53 Meeting House Lane
(01273) 729728 Open Mon-Sat
8am-6pm Sun 9am-6pm

Small friendly café, with sparse décor. A good place for breakfast in the Old Lanes as it's usually quiet in the mornings, so you should always be able to find a seat and enjoy your coffee and croissant.

Relax, eat your food and look at the plastic fish in the fish tank.

Moons
42 Meeting House Lane
(01273) 323824 Open Sun-Thur
8am-6pm Fri-Sat 8am-10pm

Busy licensed brasserie with good service. The food is unusual and

well above average for the Old Lanes. Extra brownie points for serving Horlicks, my favourite drink, as well as a wide choice of flavoured, frothy milky drinks, both hot and cold. Not your typical Brighton café.

Mock Turtle
4 Pool Valley (01273) 327380

Famous for its cakes. It looks like an old grannies tea-room with lace table cloths but don't let that put you off. If you're a cake fan, you'll think you're in heaven. They also do take-away cakes. Bring a wheelie bin.

CENTRAL BRIGHTON CAFES

Disco Biscuit*
14 Queens Road (01273) 721221
Open Mon-Wed 10am-6pm
Fri-Sun 10am-8pm

You can't miss this place as the sign outside features a 3D rocket,

and the name appears to be written in grey shit.

Disco Biscuit is one of the best cafés in Brighton just to go and chill out in. It has three big couches in the window so that you can relax in comfort, drink some coffee, eat some food and watch the world go by. The food here for the most part is excellent. They do all the normal sort of things like sandwiches, salads (try the Chicken and Bacon salad) and they do a great smoothie too. There is a good collection of magazines, and always a few of the daily rags on the table by the window.

At the time of going to press there was a rumour that they may be changing premises, so if it isn't where I say it is then you should try to track them down as it is worth the effort.

Billies
34 Hampton Place (01273) 774386
Open Mon-Sun 8am-5pm

Just up from Waitrose, at the very top of Hampton Place. Billies has developed a cult following amongst locals, largely thanks to its hash browns at which it excels. The manager is extremely friendly (though the cheeky staff beg to differ) and has one of the blackest sense of humour I've ever come across. So if you're old, fat or under five, expect some comments.

HOVE CAFES

The Sanctuary
51-55 Brunswick Street East
(01273) 770002
Open Mon 12noon-11.30pm
Tue-Sun 10am-11.30pm

Well-known and relaxed vegetarian café, with plenty of melts, salads and hot dishes of the day to choose from. In the winter this is a

good place to spend a cozy Sunday afternoon sampling the homemade cakes, while playing chess in one of the fat armchairs upstairs. In summer you can sit outside (though there's only a couple of tables) and treat it as a mellow café-bar. There's also a room downstairs that's host to many evenings of poetry and music, not to mention Junk TV's infamous nights.

Meeting Place

Hove Sea Wall Kingsway (01273) 738391 Open all year round subject to the weather

All-year-round open-air café opposite Brunswick Square. On a

warm summer morning it's a perfect spot to have your breakfast and read the paper in your pants whilst getting a suntan. In the winter when it's snowing outside and the sea is crashing over the promenade it never seems quite as busy.

KEMPTOWN CAFES

Pickwicks Café

2 St. James's Street (01273) 686273
Open Mon-Sat 9am-8pm

Pancakes and sundaes are the two items shining through the good but basic menu. The café is named after the owner, a Mediterranean Dickensian character, whose baritone voice goes to prove that smoking makes you sound like Barry White. Don't do it kids.

The Meeting Place Cafe

Pure

George Street (01273) 692457
Mon-Sat 11am-7pm
Sun 12noon-6pm

Licensed, stylish café with a
continental menu ranging from
mussels to Danish rissoles. Looks
like an arty drinking den. Why
not come here and do your
postcards as they have lots of
free ones to give away?

CAFE BARS

Grinder Café

10 Kensington Gardens (01273)
684426 Open Mon-Sat 9am-11pm
Sun 9am-6pm

Trendy young hangout in the
heart of the North Laines. The
balcony seats are coveted in
summer when you can drop your
coffee froth onto passers-by and
make them think it's seagull shit.
The food is good and not
expensive. In the evenings the
Grinder goes upbeat with a funky
selection of DJs, booze and
candles. Definitely worth a visit.

The Tin Drum

95-97 Dyke Road (01273) 777575
open Mon-Sun 12noon-11pm

Popular café-bar in the heart of
the Seven Dials, that arose from
the ruins of Brighton dingiest and
smelliest convenience store.

The house special, Zakushki, is
a selection of mouth-watering
hors d'oeuvres, ranging from
smoked salmon to pork, all served

View from Grinder Café

with rye bread, blinis and
smetalia. There's a veggie one,
too and a wide range of
flavoured vodkas to see you
through the evening. They have a
good selection of books and up-
to-date mags at the back, which
makes for a pleasant Sunday
breakfast. And ladies, sit-com
heart-throb Joe McGann is known
to drop by occasionally for a glass
of warm milk.

The Dorset Street Bar

28 North Road (01273) 605423
Mon-Sat 10am-11pm (food till
10pm except Sun till 8pm)

A visit to Brighton really is not
complete without Eggs Benedict,
a coffee and a pose outside the
fashionable Dorset.

In the heart of the North
Laines, this place is in turn a
breakfast café in the mornings,
snack bar at lunchtime and
sophisticated restaurant and
drinking den at night. And they
also do delicious mussels
and fries.

The local celebrity here is not
Steve Coogan or Nick Berry (even

Mr Cyclop enjoys a drink at The Dorset

though they do pop in), but a toothless 63-year-old character called Jack. He comes in most evenings around 5pm telling everyone it's his birthday. Every sentence starts with '*14 years ago*' and if you ask him what he's doing, he'll say – '*building a brick*'. And don't be surprised if he ends up in the ladies toilet, he's just a little eccentric.

MILES FROM ANYWHERE

Becky's Café
Top of Elm Grove
(01273) 628184
Open Mon-Sun 7am-3pm

A bit out of the way from town, and at the top of a bloody big hill. So why come here? The food is traditional British caff menu but the décor and layout provide some eccentric charm.

Originally a public loo, now adorned with red walls, large plastic gnomes and odd paintings that give the place a seedy, unintentionally surreal atmosphere.

Seek it out if you're in the area, or if you need some inspiration for your writing. The perfect setting for a sit-com.

RESTAURANTS

Blind Lemon Alley
41, Middle Street
(01273) 205151
Mon-Sun: 12pm-11pm Major
http://www.brighton.co.uk/restran
t/blindlemonalley/

Immensely popular restaurant offering cool blues and tasty southern food. Their speciality is homemade char-grilled burgers which come as meat or veggie.

The tucked away entrance makes this restaurant a bit of a find, which is good news if you like to avoid over-touristy places. Sundays are your best time to come, as local legend Phil Mills has been doing a live blues set here for years. And if you don't like it, you can throw your onion rings at him.

If you want to eat here at weekends, especially on Sunday nights, make sure you book ahead of time, since capacity is limited to 50.

News just in...
The owner 'Boss Lemon'
is still looking for the guy
who left footprints all over
the toilet walls and
ceiling. Any information
leading to his
whereabouts should lead
to a free dinner.

In a cheap copycat
style, ex-Radio 1 DJ 'The
Hairy Cornflake' has
opened up a similar
restaurant 'Deaf Leek
Trousers' just down the
road. The food is Welsh
cuisine featuring some
guy in cowboy boots
playing old Alarm songs
on a banjo. No need to
book, it's always quiet.

Cajun, American & TexMex

Old Orleans
1-3 Prince Albert Street,
(01273) 747000
Open Mon-Sat 12noon-11pm
Sun 12noon-10.30pm

Popular Cajun restaurant in the heart of the Old Lanes.

Visually it's like some awful themed pub-grub chain, but for meat-lovers the food is tremendous and plentiful, which I guess with main courses between £9 and £15, is what you'd expect.

The Red Snapper here is delicious or for the really adventurous why not wrestle with an alligator steak?

For a Special Evening

Bali Brassiere
Kingsway Court,
First Avenue, Hove
(01273) 323810

Found at the far end of Hove and done out in wicker, bamboo and plastic plants, this place is straight out of 'Love Boat' and 'Fantasy Island.' If Barry Manilow lived in Hove, he would eat here.

The setting is made complete at weekends by live music in the bar from Lola, who sits on a stool singing stuff like Nancy Sinatra and Lee Hazelwood to backing tapes and saying things like – *'If anyone has a birthday out there, come on up and we'll sort*

*you out with something reeeaal
special.'* – Mmmm, nice.

A word of warning though,
kitsch fans. Even at the weekends,
it can be pretty dead in the bar,
so I recommend it only as a place
for big groups. It'll help if you get
dressed, come on mass and
create the atmosphere yourself.

Incidentally the food is
Indonesian / Malaysian. It's good,
but a bit pricey. *'Look boss, it's de
plane, de plane'.*

Tamarind Tree
48 Queens Road (01273) 298816

Caribbean restaurant with an
authentic and chilled out feel to it.
You should plan to make an
evening of it here as the relaxed
pace means that your food may
take some time to arrive. Bring
your own drinks or try some of

their exotic juices or hot
chocolate.

The Jerk Chicken and Callaloo
Soup are particularly good and
don't be put off by some of the
more obscure ingredients, they've
written a section at the beginning
of the menu which has these
fantastic dictionary definitions like
something out of 'Call My Bluff'.
Well recommended.

Hungry Monk
Jevington near Eastbourne
(01273) 482178

This one's for the devilishly
romantic among you, and famous
for being the birthplace of
Banoffee Pie.

The food isn't cheap but the
whole set up here is utterly
charming even if it is a bit of a
bugger to find.

On arrival they escort you to a
small lounge to sample aperitifs
and bite-sized appetizers, and
make you feel like lord and lady of
the manor. After a couple of
sherries you are invited to dine in
the main room, which, with its
low ceiling, open fireplace and dim
light, contribute to the perfect
intimate romantic meal.

The portions are huge, the food
is delicious, and if you go for the
Banoffee Pie at the end, (which you
must) be prepared to leave three
times fatter than you were before
you went in.

THE HUNGRY MONK

WONDERFUL FOOD & WINE SERVED BY CANDLELIGHT

MICHELIN, GOOD FOOD GUIDE & EGON RONAY RECOMMENDED

JEVINGTON NR EASTBOURNE BN26 5QF
Telephone / Fax: 01323-482178

WITH FOUR PRIVATE DINING ROOMS

English's Oyster Bar
29-31 East Street
(01273) 327980
Open Mon-Sat 12noon-10.15pm
Sun 12.30pm-4pm

High-class restaurant with a reputation for having the best seafood in Brighton.

I decided to put this place in the special evening section since at £37.95 for a cold seafood platter (for two), it would have to be a pretty special occasion to celebrate here.

However, if you're feeling flush, this is the place for lobster, oysters and all things from the salty depths.

Oriental

Cheung's Restaurant
6B Queens Road
(01273) 327643
Open Mon-Sat 2pm-3pm and
5,30pm-12am Sun 1pm-12am

Authentically located on the first floor, this dark, seedy place always makes me think of the movie Chinatown.

The food is excellent and the gyrating tables are fun, but to anyone who's not in full possession of their faculties it can be a little daunting. Don't get stoned before you go or you'll end up eating nothing at all.

Yum-Yum Noodle Bar
22-23 Sydney Street
(01273) 683323

Refreshingly untrendy noodle bar. For the price you get a good selection of Chinese and Indonesian, and entertainment comes free courtesy of the window seat.

The food is good, and with starter, main course and tea for two for under £10 is definitely good value for money.

Worth visiting when shopping in the busy North Laines.

French

Cripes Creperie
7 Victoria Road
(01273) 327878

Done out in the style of a cosy French bistro, this is a good spot for a romantic meal.

My first dinner with Alex was here and we stuffed our faces, got drunk, smoked cigars and went home with happy bellies.

The portions are huge and the menu is so appetizing it takes a good half-hour of drooling to decide. Just add a bottle or two of Cidre Breton and the scene is set.

Make sure you book upstairs, it makes the world of difference to a truly French experience.

Crepe Dentelle
65 Preston Street
(01273) 323224
Open Mon-Sun 7pm-11pm
Fri-Sun 12noon-3pm

You can't get any more French than Chef Philippe, whose family have been tossing crêpes since the 40s. His attention to detail has turned this restaurant into a little French gem, with chequered tablecloths, candle light and Edith Piaf in the background (her music, not the corpse).

The food selection here is truly impressive, ranging from savoury pancakes to sweet, with lots of veggie options.

The pancakes have all been given French men's names like 'Crêpe Jean-Paul', which the chef is proud of. Would it work in English I wonder? '*A Donald pancake for me and my wife would like the Jeremy without onions please.*' Perhaps not.

French cider is served in the traditional bolée, for that earthy, country flavour. And to round it all up, Philippe and his wife like to warm up your bellies before you go home with a free French liquor at the end of each meal.

English
Harry's
41 Church Road
(01273) 727410
Mon-Sun 9am-10.30pm

Remember how in The Beano every week one of the characters would foil a couple of burglars ? (always dressed in black striped shirts and carrying a bag of swag), and they'd get rewarded with a slap up meal of bangers and mash at the local nosh-up? This is a posh version of that restaurant.

Italian
Alfresco
The Mikmaid Pavilion,
Kings Road
(01273) 206523
Open Mon-Sun 10am-12midnight

Looking like it's out of some 60s Italian movies, Alfresco is an enormous glass-panelled building with a commanding view of the beach.

There is a spacious round balcony on the first floor, which means you don't have to fight for a precious sunny spot during those two minutes of heat in the summer.

The food is your standard Brighton's idea of what Italian grub should taste like. Pizzas start at £5 for a Margherita and staff are very friendly.

Alforno
36 East Street
(01273) 324905
Open Mon-Sat 12noon-11pm

Immensely popular in summer as this tiny restaurant spreads outside into East Street.

Sit out, watch the world go by and enjoy the free street entertainment during the day. The best pizza in Brighton according to Alex (who should know, being from Rome).

Thai

Sada Thai Cuisine
4 Lewes Road
(01273) 677608

I haven't eaten here, but it's the best Thai restaurant in Brighton according to a couple of good friends of ours.

If it doesn't live up to your expectations, I'll give you their phone number and they'll be happy to re-emburse you.

Vegetarian

Food For Friends
18 Prince Albert Street
(01273) 202310

Stylish vegetarian café-restaurant in the Old Lanes.

There are always 3 or 4 specials every day, as well as a selection of salads and cakes, all homemade. The stir-fry with quiche is usually a pretty good option followed by the yoghurt with fresh fruit.

The notice board in there usually advertises local events with a New Age slant, and makes you wonder if owning a cat is compulsory in Brighton when you're renting out a room.

In the evening there's a BYO booze policy and it all feels very relaxed and laid back in a groovy sort of way.

Bombay Aloo
39 Ship Street
(01273) 776038
Open Mon-Thur 12noon-11pm
Fri-Sun 12noon-12am

All you can eat vegetarian Indian buffet for £4.50. Bajis, salads, dips, and main curries with rice.

Starve yourself for three days and clear them out.

Terre A Terre
71 East Street
(01273) 729051
Open Tue-Sun 12noon-10.30pm
Mon 6pm-10.30pm

Beautifully presented Nouvelle Cuisine.

From its very beginning round the corner in Pool Valley, this stylish restaurant set the scene for vegetarianism with a difference. It proved that a meal can be delicious, sophisticated and look appetizing, even without meat.

This is not a restaurant for those who want to binge, but for those who like attention to detail and care put into the dishes. Expensive and pretentious, or stylish, well-priced food? The debate continues among friends, but it's busy every night of the week. Booking is a must.

Lebanese

Kambie's
107 Western Road
(01273) 327934

This place is a real favourite. The mood always seems very lively in here and conducive for good conversation. Food-wise the meat grills are fabulous and I particularly like the batata harra (sautéed potatoes with coriander, garlic and lemon).

I came here one night when a group of us shared a seemingly endless platter of different Lebanese dishes and I cannot describe how delicious every single one was. If that's not enough, at the end of the night you get to smoke the Shiha (pronounced sheesha), which if you're not familiar with, is like the thing the caterpillar smokes in 'Alice in Wonderland'. The tobacco is flavoured with strawberries and just one puff and I'm craving Marlboro Lights again. It's bring your own

booze here as well and if you can't stay, every single dish that you can eat in, you can take away. The Falafels are particularly well-loved.

If you're in at the right time, you might be lucky enough to catch a travelling band of musicians who occasionally drop in and play Eastern European folk music. They do requests and so Alex once paid good money for them to come and serenade me while I ate. Instead, bizarrely, they played happy birthday to her, so we all joined in with the words. She now has two birthdays a year, like the Queen.

Fish And Seafood

Regency
131 Kings Road (01273) 325014
Open Mon-Sat 11am-10pm

A distinctive seafront fish restaurant that wouldn't look out of place in a 70s Carry On movie. Everything on the menu is of outstanding quality, although I'd particularly recommend their seafood platters. They're excellent value and the calamari can be chewed without having to take out a dental policy.

Regency on the seafront

THE BEST FISH AND CHIPS

Bankers
116A Western Road
(01273) 328267
Open Mon-Sun 11.30am-10pm

Classic 60's décor. Very popular for sit down and take away. The fish and chips are near-perfect and can also be cooked in Matzo meal (a Jewish alternative to batter which is definitely worth trying). They are very proud of their fish and chips here and rightly so. If you're still feeling peckish afterwards, YOU ARE A GLUTTON! But I can recommend the cheesecake.

Don't miss the indoor guttering effect above the counter. What's that all about?

Sing Li Fish And Chips
39 Guildford Road

Just up from the station, this is my local fish and chip shop which always gets a visit when there's nothing left in the fridge except for a jar of green mayonnaise and a hairy courgette. The haddock is far superior to the cod here and worth the extra 5 minutes wait. Besides, you might find another secret message on the board in there.

TAKE AWAY

Kambie's
107 Western Road
(01273) 327934
See restaurant section.

New Hong Kong
49 Preston Street
(01273) 327788

Quality food and good prices.

Nishate Tandoori
58 Preston Street
(01273) 321701
Open Mon-Sun 5.30pm-12am

Best Indian/Goan take-away, and the atmosphere in this place almost beats going out for the evening. Be ready to trade a few jokes with the staff but in particular look out for its two celebrity chefs.

One is a punk who wears a little woolly hat everywhere (including the bath apparently) and the other, David, is known locally as Woody. At one time he looked remarkably similar to the famous comedian Woody Allen, but over the years some bizarre transformation process that we don't properly understand yet has turned him into the spitting image of Peter Sellers in 'The Party'.

Piccolo
56 Ship Street (01273) 203701
Open Mon-Sun 11.30am-11.30pm

Pizzas here are good and very cheap (£4-£5), however, the hectic atmosphere and rushed service might not be to everyone's liking. I've forgotten the number of times I've used their fantastic take-away option but really should try something else apart from their Hawaiian.

Famous Moe's
Brighton (01273) 676867
Hove (01273) 779779

Well-loved take-away in Hanover. The pizzas are good value and come with a better than average variety of toppings, together with some of the creamiest coleslaw I've ever had. Go for one of their cheap deals for two people and you've got the perfect excuse to be a greedy pig and have banoffee pie after eating a whopping great pizza.

WHERE TO BUY BOOZE AFTER 10.30PM

The Tin Can
Sillwood Street Open until 11pm

The Pantry
Preston Street Open until 11pm

Southover Wine Shop
80/81 Southover Street 600402

This is one of only a few off-licences in Brighton that stays open until 11pm. Don't ask me how they wangle it, but you might just find this information a godsend one day.

If that's not enough, they stock over 40 Belgian beers, have a great selection of spirits, sell fireworks all year round and even sell bread and milk as part of a special Sunday service. Heaven in a bun.

THEY'RE HAPPY
Because they eat
LARD

Issued by the Lard Information Council

Places to Sleep

Brighton literally has hundreds of places to sleep, from hotels and B&Bs to guesthouses and hostels, and to be honest most of them are pretty similar. Despite this, in our efforts to bring you an intriguing slice of what's out there, we've tried to cover a range from the most expensive to the cheapest, the friendliest to the rudest and the simplest to the most outrageous. (And not forgetting Brighton's only camp-site).

In the more traditional B&B areas like Madeira Place prices change daily and according to what they think you'll pay. So be terribly polite but dress down for the occasion when you show up. Each room comes with TV, coffee and tea-making facilities, and breakfast is normally included in the price.

For a more complete list check the Brighton website www.brighton.co.uk, but don't expect anything more than a perfunctory description.

DEAD POSH

The Grand
Kings Road
(01273) 321188
Normal singles are £155 and normal doubles are £220 or so, add £65 if you want a sea view (save the £65 and just walk the 9.4 feet to the door and look from there).

The most famous hotel in Brighton and at £1350 per night for the Presidential suite, by far and away the most expensive. This may seem a bit steep but when you take into account that Ronald Reagan and JF Kennedy flossed their teeth in that very room, it almost makes it worth the money.

The over the top grandeur of this white palace is only matched by its facilities which include pool, health spa, hair salon and full sized indoor go-karting track which was said to be a favourite of Ronnie's. Dress code – Armani, Hugo Boss etc. No jeans unless you're royalty.

Stakis Metropole
Kings Road
(01273) 775432
Rooms with Dinner/Bed/Breakfast from
£75, Most expensive room is £480

Another grand affair situated right on the seafront between the two piers. It looks impressive enough and again caters for the more affluent ladies and gentlemen. There is a small heated swimming pool if you don't want to get greased up for swimming in the channel, three restaurants and a nightclub which is not even worthy of the phrase 'tacky as hell'.

**QUITE POSH
WITH A HINT
OF BOHEMIAN**

The Oriental Hotel
9 Oriental Place
(01273) 205050

Leave behind the world of floral carpets and gaudy wallpaper and enter the stylish surroundings of this hotel. Done out in funky colours, spattered with art on the walls, themed rooms, pine furniture and loads of plants, this place shines a light for all visitors to Brighton who want somewhere fab and groovy to stay. Popular with all ages, and of course the odd famous novel has been scribbled here too. Gets the top banana vote from 'The Cheeky Guide'.

Montpellier Hall
Montpelier Terrace
(01273) 203599
Singles from £25
Doubles from £50

More the kind of guesthouse you'd expect to find in some exotic English village than the centre of Brighton. For the Percy Thrower types it has some lavish gardens, is host to some of the rarest plants in the world and the garden furniture is made from bits of HMS Ganges. The building is reputedly haunted by a female ghost, and the king of pantomime John Morley clocked up quite a bill when he wrote his encyclopædia here. It's a phenomenal place if you care for detail.

FOR BED FETISHISTS

21 Century Hotel
21 Charlotte Street
(01273) 686450
Singles from £40 Doubles from £45

This highly acclaimed guesthouse can be found on the little street in Kemptown immortalised by the Lloyd Cole song. The rooms are individually named (Oak, Golden, Champagne) and each have different characters. Kind of like The Chelsea hotel, Victorian style. It's all a bit gaudy and over the top for me, but the rooms are spotless and refreshingly different from most of the other stuff I've seen. The brass and four poster beds in some rooms might interest those of you planning a saucy weekend.

The Lanes Hotel
70 Marine Parade
(01273) 674230
Singles from £45 Doubles from £66
4 Posters from £96

Located on the Brighton seafront, this typical hotel offers good views of the Palace Pier and the beach. There are 8 rooms here with four-poster beds and the room of the week award goes to 118 for its fabulous water-bed. Not advisable if you get seasick.

Adelaide Hotel
51 Regency Square (01273) 205286
Singles from £41 and doubles from £65 Prices drop if you stay more than one night

12 good sized rooms, all with en-suite bathrooms. If you really want the fancy stuff then go for the Regency room, which is another room with a fabulous four poster bed.

NICE AND EASY DOES IT

Dylan

Cecil House
126 Kings Road
(01273) 325942
Singles from £20 midweek

Cecil House claims to be the cheapest room on the seafront. The rooms are all quite basic but very clean and some offer great views of the West Pier. Settle down at dusk and enjoy the free show from the starlings. Red Arrows, eat your heart out.

Keehans Hotel
Regency Square
(01273) 327879
Single room and breakfast £30
Doubles vary all the way to £85 for
the top room

This family owned guesthouse is
vehemently non-smoking and they
would rather gnaw their own arms
off than let you in with a fag.

Absolutely NO Smoking!

This Means You!

If you feel the same way about
tobacco, owners John and Nancy
will welcome you in, tell you all
about their grandson (who plays
for Aston Villa) and let their floppy
old dog lick your arms. Famous
guests include Shredded Wheat
fanatic Brian Clough.
They've also got indoor parking for
bikes, which is pretty useful and
yes it's on the seafront.

Madeira House
14 Madeira Place (01273) 681115
Rates change daily

One friendly owner whose claim to
fame is that he got in the Guinness
book of records for gargling non-
stop for 14 hours. Trivia aside, the
rooms that I saw were generally a
little better than most of the others
in the same street.

Strawberry Fields
6-7 New Steine, Brighton
(01273) 681576
Prices from £22pp

Now I know what you're thinking,
what were John Lennon and Brian
Epstein doing alone in this
Kemptown B&B, and where did
they hide the body of the real
Paul McCartney? Unfortunately to
find that out, you need to check in
at the 'Paul Is Dead' guesthouse
next door as this friendly place has
no Beatles connections other than
its name.

Located in a seafront garden
square and run by a young family
with lots of energy, this is a good
place to relax and chill, especially if
you have kids as they offer a baby
listening service so that you can
get a break from it all. Clean
rooms, good views and very
reasonable prices considering the
location.

Funchal
17 Madeira Place (01273) 603975
Twin / Doubles from £28-32
No singles

One of the best B&Bs on the
street. The owners seem to like
the stories of old when B&Bs used
to be awful, and you would get
beaten with bread rollers if you
didn't finish your breakfast.

Incidentally, does anyone know
what the Capital of Madeira has
anything to do with Brighton??

The wonders of hi-tech advertising

THE CHEAPEST IN TOWN

Abbey Hotel
Norfolk Street
(01273) 729147
Rooms on floors 1-3 start at £50 per week Rooms on the fourth floor are all quite nice and start at £155 per week

Probably the cheapest weekly rental hotel in Brighton, starting at £50 per week. The cheap self-catering rooms are on the first 3 floors and on the whole are small and pretty hairy.

If it's really all you can afford, I'd rather you came and slept on my floor. The rooms on the 4th floor however are pleasant with clean bathrooms and start at about £155 for the week. Tony Benn always stays here when he's in town.

Recently some American guy totally pissed off the manageress by plonking a pair of shoes on the counter and saying in an arrogant voice – *'Have these cleaned by the morning.'* – She's still angry so if you're afflicted with the accent, tell them you're Canadian.

Aquarium Hotel
13 Madeira Place
(01273) 605761
Singles / doubles from £10 per person on a good haggle

In the heart of Kemptown and a stone's throw from the Palace Pier, this little B&B stands out as it has negotiable pricing based on what you can afford. They do a veggie breakfast on request and the rooms are clean, if a little squashed.

YOU CAN'T POLISH A TURD

George Hamilton V

27 Lower Rock Gardens, Brighton
I incorrectly thought this place was named after the Scottish Country and Western singer and thought it might be interesting. When the door opened, a rather unshaven man emerged, smelling of booze...

Me: Hello.
Him: What do you want?
Me: I am writing a guide on Brighton, and...
Him: I'm not interested.
(shuts the door)
The end.

VARIOUS OTHERS

Ambassador Hotel

22 New Steine
(01273) 676869
£23-£33 pp sharing, also has good weekly rates available

Brighton Marina House Hotel

8 Charlotte Street
(01273) 605349
Single Bed and Breakfast from £21.00 to £35.00
Double /Twin Bed and Breakfast from £45.00 to £70.00 per room

Cavalaire House

34 Upper Rock Gardens
(01273) 696899
Single Bed and Breakfast from £19.00 to £23.00
Double / Twin Bed and Breakfast from £42.00 to £58.00 per room

Ainsley House

28 New Steine
(01273) 605310
Single Bed and Breakfast from £24.00 to £30.00
Double / Twin Bed and Breakfast from £42.00 to £70.00 per room

Aegean Hotel

5 New Steine
(01273) 686547

The Quality Hotel

West Street
(01273) 220033
Single Room from £ 56.00 to £97.00
Double Room from £66.00 to £120.00 per room

Barringtons

76 Grand Parade
(01273) 604182

New Steine Hotel

12a New Steine
(01273) 681546

Amalfi

44 Marine Parade
(01273) 607956

Alvia Hotel

36 Upper Rock Gardens
(01273) 682939

B&B & GUESTHOUSE STRIPS

If you don't have any luck with the ones listed or you fancy going it alone you will find countless B&Bs and guesthouses in the following areas:

Madeira Place
Lower Rock Gardens
New Steine

Located close to the seafront but without a proper sea view. Fairly cheap, plentiful and close to just about everything.

Grand Parade

Right in the town centre, 10 minutes walk from the sea and close to the North Laines

Regency Square & Bedford Square

These squares are found just past the West Pier and the rooms overlook the sea (unless of course you get one at the back with a view of the gasworks).

HOSTELS

Baggies Backpackers

33 Oriental Place
(01273) 733740
Fax No. (01273) 733740
www.cisweb.co.uk/baggies
Dorm rooms are £10 pp and doubles are £25 (£12.50pp)
Laundry machines on site, free soap powder provided, and if you ask nicely enough Homeopathy and foot massages are provided too

Close to the West Pier, Baggies is one of the best hostels in Brighton, and while at first glance it may not seem as lively as some of the others, it's certainly the most hygienic.

The rooms all have built-in sinks and are always clean and fresh, as are the showers and bathrooms. There are two lounging-about rooms, the upstairs one has TVs and videos, the downstairs one is for listening to music and optional praying in front of the Bob Dylan shrine. If Bob is not your God, you can do the five foot crossword, eat, smoke or just hang out.

Owners Jem and Val make a real effort with visitors and will spend time with you, take you to the local pub quiz, and join into many of the late night discussions that always seem to arise here.

The hostel's oldest resident is a bear who sits in a hanging chair in the lounge. Nobody remembers when, but he just appeared after a drunken night on the pier once. Legend goes that his missing ear was bitten off by a randy French girl one night.

Friese Green Backpackers Rest

20 Middle Street
(01273) 747551
www.friesegreen.demon.co.uk
There are 9 dorms and only one double room
Prices are £10 pp for the dorms and £15pp for the double

Friese Green is just up from the Sumo bar in the club area of Brighton. This isn't the cleanest hostel in the world but it does seem to be a friendly and fun place to hang out. There are kitchen facilities provided for your own cooking, but it didn't look all that clean to me at the time and if I were you I'd rather eat out or go on a fast for a while.

Brighton Backpackers

75-76 Middle Street
(01273) 777717
Fax. (01273) 887778
www.brightonbackpackers.com
Rooms are £10 pp for the dorm rooms and £25 for a double room.

Brighton Backpackers is the typical hostel that you find in most cities around the world; loads of fun, full of colourful people and with enough reggae to keep even the most ardent Rasta happy.

I didn't find the rooms up to much, but I can't blame the staff for this as they do clean the rooms, it just seemed like everyone had thrown junk, tapes, towels and general shit all over the floor. Come on guys, you might have travelled India by dingo but clear away those smelly socks! Downstairs there is a free pool table (if you can call it that) and internet access for £3 p.h.

A WEE LITTLE STORY

I'd just been to the Arts club with Alex to see a band, and out of sheer laziness we had driven into town and parked outside Friese Green Backpackers. At the end of the night we were getting into the car to go home when I noticed a guy slumped on the pavement. He was out cold and his feet were dangling into the road. It was early March and still freezing, so I went over to see if I could wake him up. After a lot of gentle poking and shaking he came to and I asked him how he was. 'I'm alright I guess' – he slurred – 'I must have just fallen asleep on my way home' – and got to his feet. 'Can I drive you home?' – I asked – 'Naaaaa' – he said – 'I only live there.' And he pointed to the hostel 3 metres across the road and staggered inside.

The rooms are all painted different colours and most doors in the older building have Disney characters on them. You can get some discounts if you feel like a spot of painting.

Despite the odd mess, it's a lot of fun staying here and there's a good chance you'll meet some cool people who know how to party.

Walkabout Hostel
West Street

This hostel was not opened at the time of going to press. It's a chain restaurant with a hostel attached owned by some Australians and seems to be promoting all things Oz.

There was a big fuss being made by the animal rights people due to the fact that they were serving Kangaroo meat in the restaurant, but it all seemed to blow over due to the fact that Kangaroos are not an endangered species here in Brighton.

Can't tell you anything about the hostel, as it wasn't open yet, but if you want to check it out it is at the bottom of West Street down by the seafront.

CAMPING
Sheep Cote Valley
Behind the Marina off Wilson Ave (01273) 626546
Costs vary according to the season but it's around £3.90 per person per tent plus £3.50 if you've arrived by car. By foot it's only an extra £2 per night.

This is the only campsite in Brighton and I've never been there, so I don't know what it's like.

They don't like all-male groups and it's not exactly walking distance from town but it may be one of your cheapest ways of staying here aside from sleeping under the pier.

Directions for getting there are a bit complicated, so it's best to ring.

Nightlife

WATERING HOLES

Chances are that during your visit to Brighton you might be tempted to pop for a swift half somewhere, so you'll be pleased to know that we have bars to satisfy every member of society, no matter how depraved. Saying that, Rabbie's bar, Brighton's only Scottish pub, (complete with tartan carpets), has closed down. I guess there are limits to people's depravity.

FASHIONABLE DRINKING DENS

Alleycats
Brills Lane (on the seafront, opposite the Green Bagel and beside the Prodigal) (01273) 220902

This is one of the coolest and most secretive bars in Brighton, and it is surprisingly unique. The sprawling sofas, dingy red lighting and décor makes me think of some of the coffee-houses in Amsterdam. The atmosphere is definitely chilled-out and laid back, though the music can sometimes be a bit loud for talking over.

Busy at weekends, with a young discerning crowd, but not always the best place if you get claustrophobic. During the week it's much mellower. As my friend Tim said – 'If the Fun Lovin' Criminals drank in Brighton, they'd drink here'.

And may I add that in some other universe the Velvet Underground would have had the odd babycham here, too. Bars do not get any seedier than this.

The Sidewinder
St. James's Street

Young, colourful, noisy and with more character than some of the trendy ZEL pubs.

It's a bit of a trek into Kemptown, but if you're staying near there, it's a perfect starting point before you head into town clubbing. There's a big beer garden with quite a few tables and at weekends you can expect a DJ or two spinning the latest tunes. Look for the gas-piping sculpture on the ceiling.

ZEL PUBS

These are a chain of established trendy pubs found in most corners of the town. Done out in bright colours and decorated with fish-tanks, lava lamps and cool furniture, they were once unique but are now expanding at an alarming rate. Doesn't anyone want to sit on rickety chairs in quiet bars anymore?

The crowds are young and fashion conscious and these are probably the kind of pubs where Chris Evans and his TFI Friday crowd would go for a drink. Ideal as pre-club bars to get you in the mood, but be ready for a spot of over-crowding, especially at the Mash Tun and Fish Bowl. On quieter evenings, The Western Front and upstairs at the Mash Tun are the best spots. If you're on the pull, you'll probably end up somewhere like here. I recommend the chat-up line 'get your coat love, you're picked.' It never fails for me.

Shakespeare's Head
1 Chatham Place (01273) 329444

Mash Tun
Church Street (01273) 684951

Fish Bowl
East Street (01273) 777505

Western Front
11 Cranbourne Street (01273) 725656

Pressure Point
33 Richmond Place (01273) 235082

St Peter's Bar
London Road, near Grubbs

An odd little chill-out bar that looks strangely out of place down on the London Road, but I can never put my finger on why.

Pokey in a charming way and sometimes the odd DJ drops in to set the mood. It's the sort of place you'd come to plan a heist during the millennium celebrations (and I know a man who would). The faces painted in the back are worth a look too.

The Fortune Of War
157 Kings Road Arches
(01273) 205065

Long established seafront pub which gets ridiculously busy at the weekends in summer.

If you want to hang out with the crowds on the beach it's a good starting point, but it'll take you a couple of days getting to the bar. Why not bring your own beer and hang out nearby anyway?

The much-coveted window seat with sea view will not be yours unless you start queueing in February, but you could be lucky during the day when it's quieter.

The Western Front
11 Cranbourne Street
(01273) 725656

Attractive young crowd, good food and probably the best of the bunch of the Zel pubs.

Found just next to Borders by the Churchill Square Shopping Centre, the designer atmosphere is

Wait a minute, isn't that John Peel?

subdued here giving a more refreshing feel to the place. Upstairs is the best place for a natter if you forgive the mould- stain art.

Last time we were in, six phones went off in the space of 5 minutes. Ah, the sweet sounds of the upwardly mobile. Lemon with your Hoegaarden Sir?

Saint James
St. James's Street

In the heart of Kemptown, another modernised trendy pub it may be, but not in the ever-predictable style. Smart move.

The food is the same as at the Great Eastern, which means that it is a priority spot for Sunday lunch. The staff are young and friendly and promoting the place as a hang-out for students and the young-at-heart.

Last time I was in, a girl tried to pinch the book I was reading. What is the world coming to when even your trusty paperback is no longer safe from the hands of leggy young blondes?

The Sussex Yeoman
7 Guildford Road (01273) 327985

Just up from the station and painted outside in bright orange, this is a popular pub for a discerning younger crowd who don't want a pub where they have to shout over techno music. It's bright orange inside too and

makes the place look very inviting.

I walk up that hill nearly every day with my bike and when I glance in, the warmth of the place and the happy crowd inside it somehow make me feel like the kid in the old Hovis ad.

Palmers Bar
Queen Square, near the Ice Rink
(01273) 325812

Another secretive little basement bar hidden away near the ice rink. Once a brothel, now a rather special pre-club den with DJs and free tapas between 5 and 7pm.

The layout is intimate and chilled out, but there are only a few tables, so get there early for a seat as it can be a bit of a squeeze at weekends. I once saw a 50s documentary at the Cinemateque about teenagers, which had been filmed down here. Everyone had fuzzy beards and they danced like on Happy Days. The beards may have gone but otherwise things don't change much in this town.

Coopers Cask
3 Farm Road, Hove
(01273) 736945

Chocolate and lovehearts at the bar, free tampons in the ladies, table service, music mags to look at and sweets at the end of the night. Seems like someone's been doing their homework as to how to create a good atmosphere.

This charming gay-friendly bar may be quite a way into Hove, but it's well worth searching out. I particularly like the fact that the shelves here are littered with un-claimed lost property, which ends up just fitting in with the general décor of the place. I dare you to make a claim for the awful red and black cowboy hat that lives here.

I asked the barman what the large ornamental eggs by the window were all about and he just shrugged and said – *'I don't know, I hate them. Feel free to steal them.'* Go ahead punks, make his day.

WHERE TO SAMPLE A BIT OF LOCAL COLOUR

The Bugle
24 St. Martins Street
(01273) 607753

Original Irish pub down the Lewes Road with long-established folk sessions Wednesdays and Sundays and an Irish landlord with a red nose to prove it.

The Evening Star
55/56 Surrey Street
(01273) 328931

The good news is that this pub is an independent brewery that has some really outstanding beers with a new one on tap nearly every day.

The bad news is that yes, it does have its fair share of middle-aged blokes with big bellies who always win at pub quizzes and have things nesting in their beards.

At the weekend, however, the crowd is more varied and the barstaff are friendly and welcoming. Worth a visit for the beer alone.

The Colonnade
10 New Road (01273) 328728

This is the bar for the Theatre Royal next door. It's a wonderfully oddball place at the best of times and the atmosphere can range from that of a morgue to being at a Simon Callow party with everyone throwing their arms around each other, shouting – *'Darling I thought you were simply wonderful'*. Look at the signed photos on the wall ranging from Nora Batty to Jeffery Archer if you don't believe me.

The barmen look like they're out of an Ealing comedy, and the last time I was in here they were playing War of the Worlds and the guy next to me was reading a Frank Muir book.

This place is super-cool, it's just that no-one in Brighton knows it, yet. Don't be surprised to see Rod Serling sitting in the shadows.

The Hand In Hand
33 Upper St. James's Street
(01273) 602521

Another independent pub in the heart of Kemptown with the beer brewed locally on the premises. The Olde Trout (named after the landlady) comes recommended and they also do a nice line in German beer, chocolate and hard-boiled eggs.

Look out for the naked Victorian ladies on the ceiling and the sad collection of mouldy ties.

It's a very small place so don't always expect a seat, especially at weekends when its mass of regulars (middle-aged men with beer bellies who always win at pub quizzes…) are there.

Get the manager talking about his time in Bavaria and before you know it, the Lederhösen are out and the oompah* music is on.

You might like to know that:
- They do a late breakfast which is a real gem at £3.25.
- You can take home 8 pints half an hour before closing.
- This is strictly a non-pulling pub!
- Handy drinking hole for after a service at the Spiritualist Church.

Can anyone solve a mystery for me and explain where the expression 'oompah, oompah, stick it up your jumpa' comes from. Or is it actually a Lennon original?

The Heart And Hand
75 North Road (01273) 624799

This pub's obvious great selling point is its famous juke-box, which features the likes of Love, The Electric Prunes and Scott Walker. Beyond that it's just a small old-fashioned bar in the North Laines.

The staff can be pleasant but the pub does tend to sometimes attract the Brighton clique, who aren't very friendly unless you're famous or you know someone who is. Have a drink, spin some tunes but don't expect to make many friends. If they all ignore you put on the Tim Buckley track 'Once I Was' twenty times and leave. Why that track? Stick it on and you'll find out.

The Iron Duke
Bottom of Waterloo Street

One for the ghostbusters. This typical small locals' pub in Hove is only worth a visit because it is reputedly haunted by several ghosts. The bar-staff will tell you stories about strange smells and things moving around, but most of them are pretty nonchalant about it all. The first time I ever went in, one of the optics came crashing down off the wall. The landlady just shrugged her shoulders and said – *'ghosts as usual.'* Not for disco kids or the Shaggies and Scoobies amongst you.

The Regency Tavern
32 Russell Square (01273) 325652

One of Brighton's best-loved pubs where gay couples, locals and grannies sit side by side. Done out in exotic gold leaf palm trees, plastic flowers and adorned with gold cherubs, it could easily be a set out of 'The Avengers'. Even the gents is decorated with a glitterball and mirrored tiles. In spite all that, there's still something peculiarly Victorian about the place, which adds to its charm.

At weekends look out for one of the barmen, probably the most outrageously dressed man in Brighton and looking like an extra from an 80s pop video. If that's not enough, it's reputed to do some of the best pub lunches in Brighton and is also haunted by several ghosts.

WHERE TO GO FOR A GOOD NATTER

Basketmakers
12 Gloucester Road
(01273) 689006

What I love about this place is that you can leave messages inside the tins on the wall, and at the same time look for any that have been left. I hid one for you lot in the Huntley and Palmers Dundee Cake tin, though I can't guarantee it'll still be there. The one I replaced said – 'Ruth Hutt licked my face.' Make of that what you will.

The Battle Of Trafalgar
34 Guildford Road (01273) 327997

A fight in this pub is as likely as Elton John's hair growing back of its own accord. Instead, it's a relaxed locals' place with plenty of seats, bar billiards table and a small beer garden, which isn't the usual empty concrete patio and a dead cat.

The crowd here are really friendly and there's no reason why you shouldn't end up feeling like a regular after your first visit.

Look out for one of the guys in there who is the spitting image of Mr Fisher, the old headteacher out of 'Home and Away'.

The Cricketer's
15 Black Lion Street
(01273) 329472

Done out in red Victorian style furnishings with wallpaper to make your granny blush. Deserves a mention because it's one of the oldest pubs in Brighton* and gets a mention in

'Brighton Rock'. A mixed crowd of young business types, clubbers and locals make sure it's always busy, uncomfortably so at weekends. Come when it's quieter and you can see how gaudy the furnishings really are.

Many years ago, myself and a group of friends got called 'a bunch of cunts' by the grumpy landlady here for mucking about. Thankfully she's not around anymore. The body was never found…

The Great Eastern
103 Trafalgar Street
(01273) 685681

Unspoiled with any clutter except for the shelves of books at the back, this is another place to come with friends for a chat.

You need to get here early because the tables near the bar will be too cramped if there's more than four of you and there's only a few at either end of the pub. The bar staff are particularly renowned for their happy demeanour. I think this is because they are mostly made up of ex-customers who liked the place so much, they decided they might as well get paid for being in there.

Also renowned for its pub grub from Annie's Kitchen which does everything from classic to exotic food.

*The oldest pub in Brighton is reputed to be the Black Lion next door.

The Quadrant
12-13 North Street (01273) 326432

After several threats to knock it down and build a much needed drive-through burger joint, this peculiar little bar seems to be staying put for now.

In an area where crappy theme pubs are the norm, it's refreshing to find a pub that hasn't had the predictable facelift, yet doesn't feel like an old man's pub.

Two windy staircases connect top and bottom and the journey from the top bar to the gents in the basement will keep you fit if you've got a weak bladder. Looks like it should be haunted.

The Waggon And Horses
10 Church Street (01273) 602752

Like the Great Eastern but with more space to sit down. Fast becoming a fashionable haunt for familiar Brighton faces without losing its crowd of regulars.

Sit outside on a warm summer night and watch the sweaty crowds battling to get to the bar

Happy folks in the Quadrant

at the Mash Tun. Also popular with gay punters, especially on theatre nights.

AFTER-HOURS DRINKING

Sumo
9-12 Middle Street (01273) 823344
Open 8pm-1am, free before 10pm

Mixing 60s futuristic and 90s minimalism and somehow resembling the drinking den from 'A Clockwork Orange', this unique and stylish bar is well worth seeking out.

As a general policy they won't let in big groups of men, preferring instead to cater for the stylish twenties to thirties crowd who want somewhere sophisticated to meet and chat.

You can tell that a lot of thought has gone into the place, with the emphasis on subdued music, table service, and a choice of cocktails as well as a wide choice of beers. But can you name all the locations from the photos on the wall? Give all the correct answers to the barstaff, and the novelty beer-mat is yours to keep.

The Star Of Brunswick (And Vats Bar)
32 Brunswick Street East (01273) 771355 Open Monday until 1am Tues-Thu until 12.30am

Kind of your average locals' pub in Hove but boasting an after hours drinking hole called Vats Bar, which is rather special. If you want to continue boozing after 11pm without the hassle of going to a club, then this is a good place for you. It can get a bit hot and claustrophic down there if it's really busy but otherwise it has a seediness to it that I like.
Free if you go through the bar before 11pm. £1 otherwise. £2/3 at weekends depending again on whether you go through the bar or not.

Get here for last orders and save £1. That's half a cheap beer or 5 fags to a professional.

A GOOD COCKTAIL BAR

The Blue Parrot
New Road (01273) 889675

Tucked away close to the Colonnade pub, this small upstairs bar specialises in exotic and classic cocktails. Get a balcony seat overlooking the Pavilion and it's a perfect way to start or finish an evening in style. They do a terrific Piña Colada, or for the less adventurous, half a shandy with a cherry.

This place doesn't look like your average bar. The blue light and walls give it a very slick yet unpretentious look, and although there's no dress code, I always like to wear my red feather cape when I come here.

A PUB CRAWL IN HANOVER

A host of fabulous pubs await in this area of Brighton. If you're in town for more than a couple of days, I recommend you come here for a boozy night out. Your starting point is Southover Street, past St. Peters Church, opposite the Level. Yes, I know it's steep but no whinging. Walk up a short way, wait for the smokers to catch up, then start by visiting The Geese (Have Flown Over The Water).

It used to be just called The Geese, until the guy who re-painted the sign admitted that he couldn't paint geese and that he had just painted a stretch of water instead. Hence the name acquired the extra bit in parenthesis. But I digress, it used to be my local and is a small but friendly Irish pub. Opposite is The Grays, another tiny pub, famous for its superb Belgian chef and music nights. The owner has a black sense of humour and the pub's advertising slogan is pretty amusing too. Make sure you eat here some time during your stay.

Up the hill from here you'll find The Napier. For some reason it seems to be a popular haunt for disgruntled teachers, but leave them to their disgruntling because there's a great beer garden outside. Watch out for cats leaping in your pint though from the house next door. Even further up the hill your trail takes you to the trendy Pub With No Name, currently a favourite with the Skint crew. Stick on a woolly hat and anorak, give yourself a funky name like Loinclothsally and enjoy the vibe. If you have drunk enough, the idea of 'doing aeroplanes' back down Southover Street should start to be appealing by now. Keep going until you reach Hanover Terrace. Circle for a while then parachute out.

Walk down this street and look out for house number 88. A student transformed it into a big smiley face a few years ago as an art project and it's stayed like that ever since. At the end you'll find the equally hospitable London Unity, and further up, the new improved Constant Service. Steve Coogan likes the odd pint in this area, so if you see him award yourself 20 points and remember to ask him to autograph your buttocks. You will be so drunk by now, that this idea will form naturally in your head anyway.

When it's throwing-out time you must have a pizza at Famous Moe's, then crawl back home. And if it's Saturday, remember you promised to get up for 7am sharp to check out the Sunday market...

Discotheques

Home to the famous Zap Club, Skint Records and The Big Beat Boutique, Brighton's club scene boasts everything from cool underground Jazz, to Retro, House and Garage nights, as well as the biggest gay club on the South coast. Combine this with regular visits from big-name DJs, plus our own Norman Cook and Phats & Small, and it's not surprising that Brighton's clubs are packed every night of the week. What other town can boast over 30 clubs, all in walking distance of each other, and most a stone's throw from the beach? One of the very special things about Brighton clubs is that unlike so many other towns and cities, they do not merely represent that weekend escapism from drudgery and boredom. If anything, some of the best nights are mid-week, and even Sundays are starting to become fashionable. The club scene seems nothing less than a shameless celebration of living in a party town, which is probably why carnival-type music like Big Beat, Latin Jazz and 70s disco is particularly popular here. And with special events like Vavavavoom! and Wild Fruit, the scene also has a dimension of glitz and glamour that Manchester, even in its hay-day, could never have provided. **Please check local press for club-night details, as they can change on a monthly basis.**

The Beach
Kings Road Arches (01273) 722272

Found between the two piers on the seafront this spacious club, with a stylish Mediterranean flavour to its design, is among the most popular and hip places in town. Inside, the large room has been divided into main sections, including a restaurant area off to one side. The bar is huge and looks like it should have featured in James Bond's 'Goldfinger'. Since this is the current home to the famous Big Beat Boutique on a Friday, it is predictably rammed. If you're after Norman Cook you might be able to spot him at about 2am, when he usually comes on. But what with family commitments and such you can't always guarantee his presence these days. The Scratch Perverts are another favourite DJing duo here, in fact the club seems to favour a policy of having different DJs every week to keeps things from getting stale.

If I had to moan I'd say that the dance floor is a bit vague, but it's a big club so don't worry, you won't have to breakdance with someone's armpit in your face.

It's generally a friendly and unpretentious crowd down here, and it also seems quite a popular pick-up place. Get here early if you want to guarantee entry, especially at weekends. It can be a lonnnnnnggggggg wait in that queue sometimes.

"The club scene here does not wait for the weekend"

BN1 Club
Preston Street (01273) 323161
Small basement club which favours drum 'n' bass and cutting-edge house. It's all UV and white walls down there, if that's your thing. They've also got these cool little booths you can go and sit in and claim as your thrones for the night, but get there early because there's only a few. If you're up for some thumping sounds, go check it out.

Casablanca
Middle Street (01273) 321817
Specialists in Latin-Jazz and Jazz-Funk, and particularly refreshing for choosing to have live bands every night, and not just DJs. With such a strong DJ culture here, you forget sometimes what a pleasure it

is to dance to live music, especially when the bands really know how to let rip.

The club has two floors of music and it's a bit annoying that you can't take your drinks between the two, but as the top half is basically just a bar (with a naff car theme), I'd recommend sticking to the downstairs bit. Shame that the dance area is between the bar and the exit, but if the funky music and those horns don't move you to dance, you're in the wrong club.

The Catfish Club
19-23 Marine Parade
Underneath the Madeira Hotel, this oversized school hall has been home for many years to an evening of Northern Soul and Motown.

This is generally a place for an older crowd, with regulars in their twenties and thirties coming to indulge their passion for this music. The venue is awful, but it seems to be the only place in town where absolutely anything goes on the dance floor. So if you're tired of practising those high-kicks at home you now know where to go.

The Core Club
12-15a Kings Road (01273) 326848
Tiny basement club next to Dr Brighton's on the seafront, with a heavy slant towards Garage, Electronic, pure Pop and weird shit.

Attracting Brighton's oddball

community of non club clubbers, this 100 capacity venue manages to somehow squeeze in the occasional small-label band pushing down the capacity to about 12. Being such a small place, if the music is too loud there's nowhere to escape, and it does tend to occasionally attract lost beer boys who usually only manage a couple of tracks before buggering off. Fridays come recommended, especially if there's a band whereas Saturdays still leave a lot to be desired. Look out for the bar staff doing sequential dancing.

The Cuba
160 Kings Road Arches
(01273) 770505

Sandwiched between three successful clubs down on the seafront, this place suffers a bit from an identity crisis, which is a shame because the layout is in some ways far better than many of its neighbours.

Like the Zap, this club's design is split level with arched brick ceilings, and set out with wooden floors and plenty of cool seating areas. It should be a great club, so why the queues for the other clubs on the seafront stretch into eternity while this place is half-full during the week is a mystery. At weekends however, it's pretty packed for popular Hard-House and Garage nights.

Escape
Marine Parade (01273) 606906

This cool Art-Deco building done out in mint-choc chip and over-looking the seafront is still one of the most successful clubs in Brighton. With winning formulas for music and promotions, it attracts a young, to very young, horny crowd, who

love getting tarted up and partying. The dance floor is downstairs in the Candy Room while upstairs is the bar. Expect two floors of dance music and anything that's currently in vogue. It's also the first Brighton club to have all-girl DJ nights and in recent years has claimed the highest place among all Brighton clubs in the Muzik Magazine national chart.

If you look above The Escape you'll see there's a flat on top with a commanding view of the beach and, in particular, the phone box in front of the club. These two guys I know, Mark and Bruce used to live up there, and some nights after the club had almost cleared out, they'd ring up the phone box, wait for some pissed-up clubber to answer, take a note of how he was dressed, and then play these weird 50s adverts down to the line to him. It would start with some cheesy music and then go –

'Hi, and welcome to the world of Lux soap, a new powder that'll get your clothes whiter than white.' – and then a different voice would say – *'You are wearing a blue hat.'*

Click

The Event 2
West Street (01273) 732627

The largest club in Brighton, specialising in chart, disco and dance, and popular with students and weekend revellers. Don't take the place too seriously and you'll have a good time.

At weekends the dance floor is a sea of Top Man and Top Shop fashion, and has its fair share of virgin clubbers. It is of course a blatant meat-market, but the nights are generally cheap, unpretentious and unashamedly glitzy.

Also host to occasional big-name gigs and special London club nights such as Escape from Samsara.

The Gloucester
Gloucester Place (01273) 688011

It's been around since 1692 and still going strong. Expect cheap and cheerful nights with every taste catered for, from House and Indie, to 70s and 80s nights.

Hardly at the cutting edge of fashion, but there's plenty of space inside and a dance floor straight out of Saturday Night Fever. The crowd seem unpredictable at the best of times, especially during the week. Sometimes it's full to capacity, other nights there's just a few Goths sat in the corner eating free jelly. Also home to the bi-monthly Vavavavoom when the whole place gets redecorated for their wild theme nights and the sexiest people in the South descend upon this humble club.

The Honey Club
214 Kings Road Arches (01273) 202807

Popular students' haunt during the week and packed at weekends for its popular house nights. I've got to be honest, I don't like the place much, it doesn't have a lot of character and feels like a cheap imitation of The Zap. It's just that with too many smoke machines, few places to sit and the crowd parading the latest High Street fashions, it all seems a bit naff to me. But it's busy every night, so it must be doing something right.

Lady Laverne outside the Honey Club

Saturdays are a must, however, just to witness the lovely Lady Laverne turning away punters at the door for being too ugly.

The Hungry Years
8-9 Marine Parade (01273) 604409

Located almost opposite the Palace Pier, The Hungry Years is Brighton's link to the slowly diminishing Metal Community.

Every weekend is Rock heaven as ageing Rockers headbang their way through a load of metal classics. During the college year however, it can still be very busy, very entertaining and very loud.

Forever teetering on the edge of self-parody, I'm just waiting for the day when the gay crowd

What do you mean you don't like Marillion ?

descend upon it and turn it into the best kitsch night in Brighton. Until then, it's shirts off, hair down and let's see those air guitars.

The Jazz Place
Ship Street (01273) 321692

Noted for its fabulous Salsa and jazz music, spun by resident DJ Russ Dewbury, this popular but tiny basement club is a real gem. It is small, think your bedroom with a bar, and you can't exactly slip off into the corner with someone, but tangoing cheek-to-cheek is the next best thing.

Intimate, relaxed and with a happy, friendly crowd, you should have a fabulous time here. If you love the music, listen to Surf FM on a Sunday for more of the same.

The Joint
West Street (01273) 321629

Done out in quite a kitsch style with heavy red lighting and leopard fur seating, it's not surprising that classic nights such as Turned Out

Nice Again and Dynamite Boogaloo should end up here. This small basement club is usually a drum-machine free zone and plays everything from 60s Soul and R 'n' B to Indie, Soundtrack and Easy Listening. There are plenty of seats and a good L shaped bar where you get served fairly quickly. Expect a mixed crowd ranging from Small Faces lookalikes and Mod chicks to weekend revellers. Sharp outfits are de rigueur at weekends if you don't want to be stared at contemptuously.

The Ocean Rooms
Morley Street (01273) 699069

Probably the strangest club in Brighton. Its three floors include a cocktail bar upstairs, a large restaurant area on the ground floor and a dance floor downstairs.

The cocktail bar is very decadent, with poufs, soft red lighting and the biggest red-velvet settee I've ever sunk into. Both this and the restaurant, with its huge tables and plenty of seats, are perfect chill-out areas and conducive to good conversation. It's only the dance-floor downstairs that lets them down, as it's still a bit stuck in the 80s.

Mid-week the club attracts students and a young crowd, while at weekends it's an older, dressier crowd that descend, but you can't help get the feeling the place is still searching for a real identity.

If you want a club where you can relax and chat in style without worrying about over-bearing noise and elbows in your beer, it's worth a visit, but don't expect it to always be busy. This could easily be one of the best clubs in Brighton. Keep your fingers crossed for the future.

The Paradox
West Street (01273) 321628

Taking itself slightly more seriously than The Event, this place tends to attract a slightly older and more image-conscious crowd. The interior is done out with mirrors and carpets and has a pretty big dance-floor, for lots of arm-waving.

Full of clubbers in their late teens, the music ranges from chart and disco to hi-energy and 70s-80s themes. Queueing at the bars at weekends can be a nightmare though, and I've waited up to half an hour to be served before.

Next door is their other club, the Barcelona, which opened to their older crowd who got fed up with sharing a dance-floor with young kids. For most nights it's for the 25 or over crowd, so please bring an Ikea catalogue as proof of age.

The Paradox is also home to Wild Fruit one Monday a month, when it's hi-energy music, drag heaven, and an excuse to dress up in your girlfriend's sexiest clothes. (See special club night reviews)

The Pavilion Tavern
Castle Square (01273) 827641

This place has always been a popular spot for Indie music, ever since Brighton's infamous Basement Club committed suicide after one of the DJs left a Shed 7 record playing all night by mistake.

The Pav Tav (as it's known) is basically a function room above a pub, but has enough character to suit the style of the club nights here. Subdued lighting, a wide bar and a few sofas make it intimate and friendly, and the Indie nights I've been to have always been busy, with a crowd eager to dance.

Friday nights have, for a while now, been home to Fresh, a Lesbian night which is gaining ever-increasing popularity. Come Saturday, it's back to The Smiths, Oasis and 200 nicotine-stained and pasty-faced kids in need of a good square meal.

Pressure Point
Richmond Place (01273) 235082

Upstairs above the pub, this small venue has a good sound system and puts on some interesting club nights (and gigs). Don't expect much in the way of character though, as it is still little more than a small hall with a bar and a stage. Think of it as an after-hours drinking place with good music but nowhere to sit.

The Shrine
Dyke Road (01273) 208678

This converted church just around the corner from the Clock Tower is another club in Brighton that seems to constantly suffer from an identity crisis, having the occasional club night that drifts in and out of vogue.

The bar downstairs is a bit grim, and if I was honest, the boxy dance floor space upstairs is a bit shabby too. Saying that, I haven't been for a while, so maybe it got re-furbished and no one told me.

Volks Tavern
Madeira Drive (01273) 682828

Found on the promenade just to the east of the Palace Pier, this is essentially a pub with a few tables and a small dance floor area. It has however been home for many years now to an evening of cool 60s sounds from The Bubblegum Factory and is still going strong. This club night is usually on a Saturday, mixing soundtracks with

To all the women I've loved before

more jazzed up styles. Stick on your favourite flowery shirt and corduroy wig, and come down and swing your pants.

The Underground
West Street

Poky basement club where all the die-hard Indie-Goths come and slouch around at the weekend. First club I ever went in when I moved here, and last I ever want to go back to.

Mind your head on the way in as some of the little fellows like to hang down from the ceiling.

The Zap

Kings Road Arches (01273) 202407

Under the arches, right down onto the beach, this is probably Brighton's most famous club. Home to some of the UK's top club nights which have featured the latest and the greatest on the decks, from Carl Cox to Boy George. Although no longer top dog, and despite its ever-growing grottiness, The Zap is still enormously popular with the more serious clubbing crowd, and the weekend (and weekday) queues still prove it. The Pussycat Club on a Friday is now in its fourth year and still going strong.

As you enter inside this cavernous space there's a big dance floor area and stage to your left surrounded by plenty of balcony space and a chill-out room upstairs, with a separate bar and a few chairs and tables.

Currently favouring House, Garage and 70s music, The Zap pulls a crowd of glammed-up young starlets that have made it past the tough entry examination at the door. Watch out for the floor in there, accidentally drop your tank top in some spots, and it will forever smell like a beer-towel and ashtray.

SPECIAL CLUB NIGHTS

Vavavavoom!

At the Gloucester
Alternate months on Wednesday

Every other month The Gloucester is host to one of the best nights in Brighton. Based on 50s burlesque tradition, Vavavavoom! features saucy cabaret acts, strippers, go-go dancers, live music, guest singers and other surprises.

COMING SOON TO A VAVAVAVOOM NIGHT NEAR YOU

キミ
ヌシホ
ヤキミ
ヌホヤテ

REVENGE
OF THE FURRY NIPPLE II

WITH
STELLA STARR AS THE NIPPLE TASSEL SWINGING HOT MAMA

Each event is themed and you are strongly urged to dress up for the occasion to keep the mood. Previous themes have included voodoo horror, circus freaks and Elvis. Not for the raincoat brigade, the emphasis is on sexiness, fun and definitely no inhibitions.

Past highlights include the three-breasted lady and live mixed-sex wrestling. And I do look good in a smoking jacket, fez and slippers, even though I say so myself. Best club night in Brighton without a doubt.

Wild Fruit
At the Paradox
First Monday of every month

Well established and glamourous night for extroverts and anyone who fancies sticking on a frock and false eyelashes or anything that glitters. This club night was originally targeted exclusively at the gay scene but word got around at how good it was, so they opened up their doors to everyone. Still predominantly a gay crowd, this is an evening of serious flirting, high camp, dressing up and Uplifting House and Garage music.

Pussycat Club
Every Friday at the Zap

In its fourth year now and seeming more popular than ever, this groovy night out has a mixed gay-straight dressed-up crowd, determined to prove that this is the best Friday-night club in Brighton. The music is Hard Uplifting House and glam attire or fancy dressed is strongly recommended.

AT A GLANCE

Big Beat – The Beach
Chart/Disco/High-Energy – The Paradox or The Event? You decide.
Drum 'n' Bass – BN1 Club
Easy Listening/Soundtrack – The Joint
Goth/Industrial – The Underground or The Gloucester (at a push)
Hip-Hop and Breakbeat – Pressure Point and sometimes The Jazz Place
House and Garage – The Zap, The Escape or The Cuba
Indie – The Pavilion Tavern
Jazz/Funk/Salsa – The Jazz Place or The Casablanca for live Jazz/Funk
Northern Soul/Motown – Catfish or The Joint at the weekends
Reggae – Roots Garden at the Jazz place or The Pressure Point
Rock – The legendary Hungry Years
70s/80s – Popular as a mid week alternative at a host of different clubs, try The Zap or the Gloucester
60s Retro – The Pavilion Tavern
60's Soundtrack/Psychedelic/Jazz – Long established at the Volks Tavern
Weird Electronica and Underground Pop – The Core Club

Stella Starr's Step-by-Step Guide to Making Your Own

Nipple tassels!

You will need:~ a pencil, some Spirit Gum, scissors, needle & thread, some thin leather patches, cotton binding, small curtain tassels, strings of sequins + a small round tin & Super Glue!

① Take a small round tin (or any round object roughly the same diameter as your nipples) & draw round & cut out the circles of leather.

② Cut into the middle of each circle & form cones!

overlap

Glue this together with Super Glue...

...carefully!

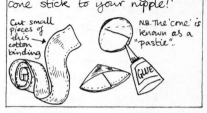

③ Cut off the right amount of cotton binding to cover inside of each cone. Glue. The binding helps the cone stick to your nipple!

Cut small pieces of this cotton binding

N.B. The 'cone' is known as a "pastie".

GLUE

④ On the outside of each cone carefully stick lengths of sequins cut to fit (or sequinned material – in fact, use your imagination – any kind of material will do!)

fake fur leopardskin ones are grrreat fun!

gold lamé will shimmer nicely!...

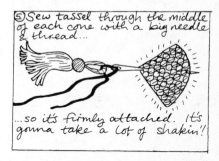

⑤ Sew tassel through the middle of each cone with a big needle & thread...

...so it's firmly attached. It's gonna take a lot of shakin'!

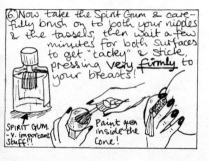

⑥ Now take the Spirit Gum & carefully brush on to both your nipples & the tassels, then wait a few minutes for both surfaces to get "tacky" & stick, pressing very firmly to your breasts!

SPIRIT GUM. v. important stuff!!

Paint inside the cone!

⑦ Now – Shake it, Baby, Shake it!...

You can make any shape nipple tassels – hearts, stars etc!

Peel them off carefully (like removing a plaster!) & clean your nipples with SURGICAL SPIRIT & COTTON WOOL. Use them again & again! SAx

Cinemas

See the latest Hollywood movie Friday night, a David Lynch season on the Saturday, then a documentary about SM on the Sunday. Here's how.

WHERE TO SEE THE LATEST BLOCKBUSTER

The Odeon
**West Street next to The Event
0870 5050007**

The biggest cinema in the town centre. Handy spot if you fancy seeing a movie before you go clubbing. Due to be upgraded soon with more screens, and through popular demand they'll be stocking their curried tomato popcorn again soon*.

Virgin Cinema
The Marina 0541 555145

Eight screens with all the latest movies from Tinseltown. You won't find anything too adventurous in their billings, but if you like modern swanky cinemas, you won't be disappointed.

---

*The reason popcorn is eaten at the cinema is because when feature films first started to be shown, the cinema owners were afraid that their audiences would get impatient and hungry if made to sit still for over an hour. So they racked their brains for the cheapest, simplest solution which turned out to be popcorn, which naturally they gave out free. Funny how things change isn't it?

Besides, if the film's crap you can take a walk on the Marina breakwater and pretend you're in 'The French Lieutenant's Woman'.

ABC
East Street (01273) 202095

Another one that's being bulldozed soon, but they wouldn't tell me when. If it's still open, I can recommend it as the cheapest option if you want to see a blockbuster.

There are only three screens so the choice is limited, but if you prefer the old-style cinemas to the shopping malls many of them are becoming, then this is for you.

'A slush puppy and a bag of jelly babies please Missus.'

INDEPENDENT CINEMAS

Duke Of Yorks
**Preston Circus (01273) 602503
www.picturehouse-cinemas.co.uk**

Found at the end of London Road, the building is yellow and has a large pair of stripy legs sticking out from over the balcony. It's easy to miss however, as all the houses on the street have copied the idea, and now there are hands, elbows and feet sticking out all over the place, as far as the eye can see.

This is a long-established independent cinema, which shows a fairly wide selection of cult, arthouse and world films,

Duke Of Yorks Theatre

alongside the blockbusters. They have a bar upstairs and do some really nice grub, a change from the usual junk food. The auditorium looks fabulous, and the seats are the most comfortable in Brighton, although it can get a bit chilly in winter sometimes.

I thoroughly recommend a visit here for movie enthusiasts. If you fancy seeing one of their late-night screenings at the weekend, buy your tickets in advance, as they often sell out.

The best day to come to the Duke of Yorks is Monday. Why? Because it's their cheapest day of the week and on the hour, 6pm-12am, the legs do the Can-Can.

Cinematheque
9-12 Middle Street (01273) 384300
cinematheque@yahoo.com

Upstairs at the media centre, this sixty-odd-seater cinema has established itself as the place for cutting edge, rare and experimental films.

Run by Ben, Michael and Adrian of the Richard O' Brien appreciation society, it is a melting pot of documentaries, cult movies, rare screenings and shaved heads. Everything from UK horror seasons to US underground and rare oldies get aired here. Some of the stuff they show here is real cutting-edge cinema and you will not see it in your video shop six months later. If all that sounds too heavy for you, how about a Buster Keaton special?

129

CINEMATHEQUE

THE INNER WORLD OF THE ENGLISH
1939-1979: UK HORROR SEASON
PLUS FRINGE FESTIVAL + CIRCUIT
BREAKER + VERHÄNGNIS + MORE

THEATRES

Brighton's Little Theatre Company
Clarence Gardens (01273) 205000

Tucked behind the Pull and Pump and down a little pathway, this converted chapel is in an idyllic spot for a theatre.

The company put on about 12 shows a year, predominantly re-makes of established works ranging from Irvine Welsh to Stoppard.

Avoid the back seats if you do go, there are low slung beams that can obscure the view and spoil it.

If you're wondering about the cult-like photo of Donald Synden in there – he is one of the founding fathers. At least that's what the guy in white robes told me.

Check local press for details.

New Venture Theatre
Bedford Place (01273) 746118

This converted school does about 9 productions a year. They cover more difficult and unusual plays. For fans of amateur theatre, done with luvvie gusto.

Komedia
Gardner Street (01273) 647100
www.komedia.dircon.co.uk

It's a blessing to have a theatre in town that doesn't churn out the usual old cobblers, year in, year out. Instead, The Komedia has new plays, live music, cabaret and comedy on nearly every day of the year.

The prices can be a bit intimidating at times, but it's usually worth a gamble, the quality of what's on here usually being pretty good. There's a more informal 230-seater cabaret bar in the basement as well as the theatre upstairs and plans for a rotating restaurant at the top.

Theatre Royal
New Road (01273) 328488

For the more conservative theatre-goer. It's the usual souped-up collection of farces, thrillers, Shakespeare and musicals, but for that authentic old style theatre experience you can't beat it. The auditorium is fabulous; plush red seats, 20p binoculars, old style viewing boxes, and you can still smoke in the bar during the intervals. I once saw Barbara Windsor in the nude here but that's another story.

Dress code – loafers, slacks and a cardie. Monocle optional.

A post-play bevy in The Colonnade next door is, of course, compulsory.

Akademia
14-17 Manchester Street
(01273) 622633

Student hangout which doubles up as a theatre and café. The food is good and, to fit with student lifestyle, cheap and plentiful. As well as the odd bit of theatre, expect to find good comedy nights here, too. And it's not just exclusive to students, so you don't need to sneak in disguised as Rick from 'The Young Ones'.

Sallis Benney Theatre
University of Brighton, Grand Parade (01273) 643010

This place is as dead as a dodo for six months, but out of the blue it will have live music, plays and dance, and then suddenly go back into hibernation again. It's like some drunk relative who's been woken up at a party and dances their way across the living room only to collapse unconscious in the kitchen moments later.

CULT & DIY TV
Junk Television
For details call
(01273) 727358 / 882313
junktv@thepentagon.com

I've seen episodes of 'Monkey' and 'Fantasy Island', madcap home-made films, animation, adverts with funny overdubs, silly competitions and loads more at their nights. Always held downstairs in the Sanctuary café (see Food Section) a few times a month, be ready to expect an evening of bizarre goggle-box programmes.

Things are quiet in summer as they usually take their show on the road, so September to May are the best times to catch them here. If you've made the odd film in the past, bring it down or send it to them and get it viewed. Brighton's answer to Exploding Cinema.

A few favourites from the past:

Blue Movie – '*A porn film shot from the distance of 1 inch.*'
Bring Along Your Worst Vinyl – '*An evening of musical horror*'
It's A Jazz Thing – '*Free Jazz meets quantum physics and someone gets stuck inside his charity shop coat.*'

NIGHTLIFE

GAMBLING

The Grosvenor Casino
Queens Road (01273) 326514
Open until 4am

Step into this 80s movie set situated just across from Brighton station. It's free to join and entrance is also free, but it takes 24 hours for them to validate your ID. The roulette tables start at 25p a bet, and the Pontoon and Poker start at £1 but there are other tables with higher stakes, if you're feeling brave.

It's fun to hang out and watch the professionals in action. Besides, can you really resist getting £10 worth of 25p chips and going mad on the roulette wheel, just for one night?

Along with all this you get a place to drink until 2am, cheap drinks, and the cheapest (and earliest) breakfast in town. Six of us had breakfast in there one night with a couple of drinks and it only came to £13! And did I really hear the girl say – 'Good Evening Mr Paradise' – to one of the regular gamblers as we were leaving?

The Greyhound Track
Nevill Road, Hove (01273) 204601

Now all the Parklife nonsense is over, you can go to the dogs and have a laugh without feeling that you have to be postmodern about it. It's a few quid to get in, and the minimum bets are a pound. Forget trying to figure out how the betting works, just pick the dog with the silliest name, use the touts just outside for better odds, and watch out for the lasagne.

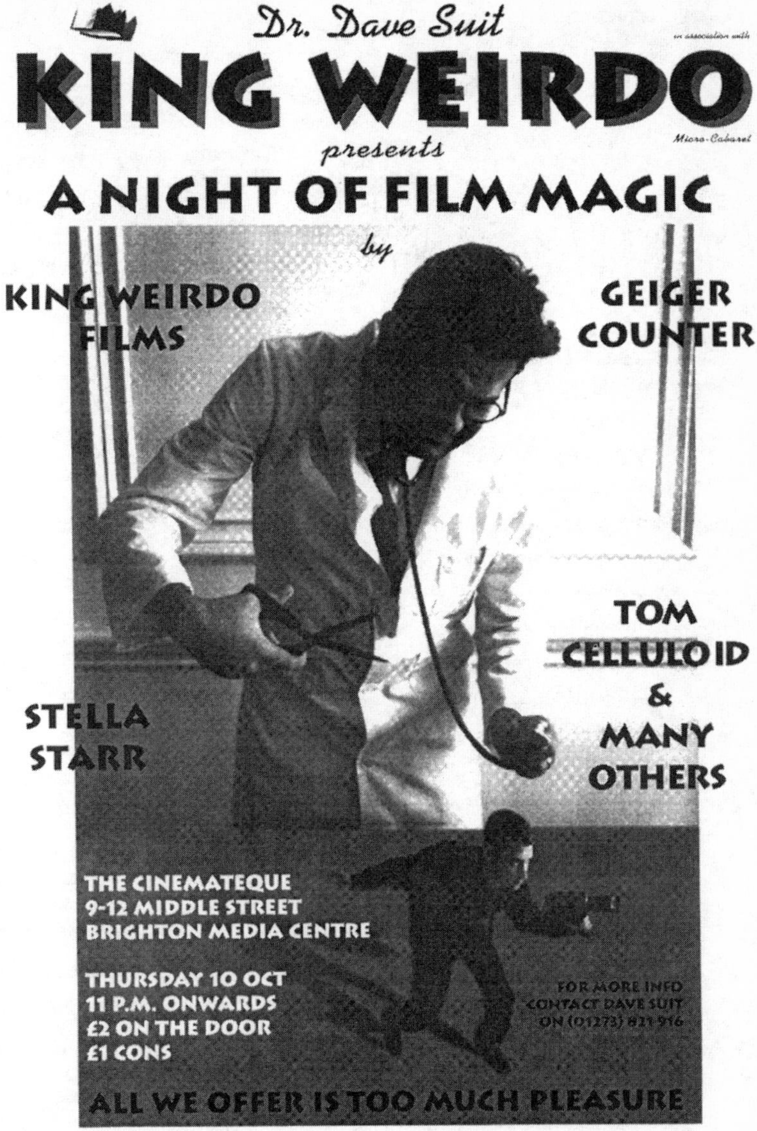
Dr. Dave Suit
in association with
KING WEIRDO
Micro-Cabaret
presents
A NIGHT OF FILM MAGIC
by
KING WEIRDO FILMS
GEIGER COUNTER
TOM CELLULOID
&
MANY OTHERS
STELLA STARR
THE CINEMATEQUE
9-12 MIDDLE STREET
BRIGHTON MEDIA CENTRE
THURSDAY 10 OCT
11 P.M. ONWARDS
£2 ON THE DOOR
£1 CONS
FOR MORE INFO
CONTACT DAVE SUIT
ON (01273) 821 916
ALL WE OFFER IS TOO MUCH PLEASURE

Music

LIVE MUSIC VENUES

There are plenty of places in town for seeing live music, especially in pubs and clubs. For some odd reason though, this town has always suffered from a lack of medium sized venues. Why this is, is a total mystery. If you want to make a shrewd business investment, open up a 400 capacity venue in the centre of town and watch the pennies roll in. Listed below are the venues that currently put on gigs on a regular basis.

The Lift
Queens Road (01273) 779411

This tiny but magical venue is tucked away, half way up Queen's Road above the Pig in Paradise.

Countless evenings have been spent here, some awful, some astonishing. I have seen gigs, spoken word events, shambolic cabaret and the odd fire. It is also regular host to different jazz bands, which to my shame I've yet to experience. Check the board outside for what's on that day, phone or sneak a look in the local press.

The Arts Club
The bottom of Ship Street (01273) 727371

Don't worry about the confusing door policy here, you do need to be a member but they always let you into the ballroom for special events.

The room itself is a beautiful setting for music, especially the more atmospheric variety, it's just a shame that the bar in there is crap. One night it could be Blues, Jazz or Salsa, the next electronic wizardry and lo-fi for lovers of underground stuff. Watching the Canadian 12-piece 'Godspeed You Black Emperor!' playing there was sublime. Trying to join in with line-dancing classes however was something quite different.

The Brighton Centre

Big names for silly prices. This is where you'll see the likes of Boyzone, Metallica and Billy Graham. But not necessarily on the same bill.

The Pressure Point

Reasonable venue with a better-than-average PA system when used properly. Expect the odd local bands, your typical touring NME up-and-coming darlings and special club nights.

The Free Butt
Phoenix Place

Hidden behind the Phoenix Gallery on Lewes Road among the old colourful Brighton squats. Once *the* place to see garage bands in a poky little room with a crap PA. Then some bright spark decided to chuck loads of money in and improve everything. The result: a bigger room, better PA and yet inevitably some of the old magic got lost forever. But it's still a good spot to see local talent for a few hundred pennies.

THESE GUYS PUT ON GOOD GIGS

Disastronaut

Unashamed self-publicist and once described as the worst DJ in Brighton, Jeff's gigs range from the shambolic to the occasionally sublime. For a real taste of Brighton, check out one of his nights at The Lift or the Arts Club (host to his nearly famous Slack Sabbath on a Sunday).

Jeff can be spotted round town in his butler outfit and Remains Of The Day hat. He is also in several hundred bands of his own, which he will be more than happy to tell you about. See him perform before he finally goes mad. **For info call (01273) 779144**

Melting Vinyl
www.alt-brighton.co.uk/Alt-brighton/meltingvinyl.html

The hard-working efforts of Steve and Anna means that we get treated to a stack of gigs each month from the likes of Will Oldham, Kreidler and Bis.

Everything from Garage-Pop to weird Electronica comes under their wings. You can check their website to get a flavour of what they promote and to check for up and coming gigs.

Geiger Counter
Geiger Counter HQ
(01273) 731743

Tipped to be the next Dr Who, Geiger Counter puts on the occasional film and music events in Brighton. Responsible for the fabulous Pioneers Of Electronic Music Festival in 1998, he has since put on a host of evenings of experimental super 8 films with electronic soundtracks from the likes of Fridge to the theremin tweakers Louis et Bébé Baron.

HOW TO FIND OUT WHO'S PLAYING

All the local magazines will give you a run-down on who's playing, and where. (See reviews).

Some of the best places to pick up information are the record shops themselves, which might have posters for last minute and low-key gigs. Edgeworld Records is particularly good for finding out titbits of information on all things underground.

WHERE TO GET TICKETS

Edgeworld
For Electronica/lo-fi affairs

Rounder Records
For bigger gigs and special club nights (01273) 325440

HMV
61-62 Western Road
(01273) 747221

Dance 2 Records
129 Western Road
(01273) 220023 / 329459

LOCAL RADIO
Southern FM

Did someone mention Alan Partridge?

Surf FM 107.7

During the daytime it's not a million miles from Radio1 (except without the odious Chris Moyles). In the evenings however, they play some way out cool dance tunes, keep you in touch with what clubs and gigs to go to and are invaluable during the festival. I really like the Latin-American stuff they play on Sunday afternoons but my favourite show is Totally Wired. This is on 11pm-1am every day of the week and plays stuff from the likes of Cornelius and Captain Beefheart. To find out what's on in Brighton tune in between 6.30 and 7pm weekdays. Fans of Skint Records might like to know they do a show Sundays between 9 and 11pm.

Of course by the time this goes to print it might all have changed, been bought up by Chris Evans and confined to playing Ocean Colour Scene 24 hours a day. Remember how Nazi Germany started.

A Short Essay On Busking

If you're thinking of earning some extra cash, this can be a fun way of doing it. Don't expect too much enthusiasm from the locals however, there are a lot of regular buskers to compete with. The foreign language students will not be your best market either. Generally they will stand around for ten minutes, have their picture taken with you and then bugger off to MacDonalds without paying anything. I recommend that you sell your soul and aim for the tourists.

Your best bet is to go for the novelty approach and make yourself stand out for the day-trippers who will see you as a 'unique experience', even if you have been standing outside the pier for the past ten years hammering nails up your nose. Look for a good spot where a lot of people are passing by you. Ideally somewhere where they might stop and watch (ie not a busy high street). Why not look around for some empty shops to stand in front of? If you stand in a doorway quietly strumming  your guitar and singing Nick Drake songs to your feet then you will join another twenty hopefuls around the Lanes. Don't be afraid to make a fool of yourself, people will pay good cash for this. Be bold in asking for money but don't be pushy. If you have an act with another person, have one of you going into the audience now and again with a hat. Some punters are put off paying by the sheer exposure of leaving the crowd to drop those precious coins in your box.

Use the odd bit of audience participation. It will draw interest from the crowd, as they thank the lord that they weren't picked. I was unlucky enough to have been selected as straight man last year for an escapologist outside the pier whose entire act seemed to have been based on watching Bottom a couple of times. He humiliated me with awful jokes and spent twenty minutes just putting on a straightjacket and then taking it off again. But by his shouting and confidence he pulled a big crowd and made a lot of money in a very short time, so good luck to him. Saying that, if I ever see him again I will kill him.

One final tip. If you have a pet, bring it. Buskers with animals make shit loads of money. Bring along your stick insect collection and your woolly mammoth. The more unusual the better. Look out for the guy with the grey rabbit in the Old Lanes. I don't know how he keeps it from running away, it must be nailed to something. But he knows he's on to a good thing.

BUSKING DONT'S

Didgeridoo

No longer a novelty.

Bongo Drums

These have a habit of irritating anyone with a shop or office within a one mile zone of you and will make you extremely unpopular.

The Penny Whistle

All love of this instrument has been beaten out of me over the years by countless buskers who think that you will be fooled by them simply blowing and randomly moving their fingers up and down.

WHERE TO BUSK IN SUMMER

East Street
(opposite Al Forno's restaurant, just past the taxi rank)

In Summer and during the May festival it's a prime spot. For some reason the acts here always seem to feature somebody playing the double bass. Of course when you go it'll be a juggler and you'll realise the awful truth that I've never actually been to Brighton and all of this is made up.

If you want this coveted spot, I'd get there early and be ready for a bloodbath.

Brighton Place
(opposite Donatello's in the heart of the Old Lanes)

Probably the second most coveted spot in Brighton. Every Summer there's a full-on pan-pipe band who haven't seen the 'Fast Show' yet. Get there early.

Where Kensington Gardens Meets Sydney Street

There used to be a guy playing Blues guitar here, but you don't see him around anymore so make the best of it. This spot has a big turnover of pedestrians but there's also a lot of retailers around so don't make it too noisy. And don't expect the punters to stick around, there are too many alluring shops around you. It's a good spot if you have a short novelty act like setting fire to yourself.

Gardner Street

It's a car-free road on a Saturday and quite conducive to the odd spot of busking.

Don't play Oasis on your acoustic guitar here though, it's very predictable and you will have a fairly discerning audience. Be different, play Fatboyslim on a Bontempi organ. Try and make the buggers smile.

Down On The Seafront

The closer to the Palace Pier you get, the more punters you will get. But it can get noisy down there too, especially by the roundabout. I'd find a compromising spot between the two piers and be prepared to deal with a few lager louts. Many years ago, a group of us used to busk right down on the seafront opposite The Beach. That was a great spot but we did suffer from getting a crowd up on the promenade, who stood, looked down, clapped and then left without paying. Saying that, if anyone *had* thrown money down, I'd probably still be recovering from the bruises.

WHERE TO BUSK IN WINTER

You can't busk inside Churchill Square as the Gestapo will throw you out but you can go to the Imperial Arcade where at least you're out of the rain and cold. Plus the acoustics are great there. Don't expect a huge turnover of pedestrians and don't spend all your earnings on novelty items from the Condom Store.

You could also try Market Street by Hanningtons, which is also sheltered and gets very busy, especially at the weekend.

THE BRIGHTON MUSIC SCENE

It is a well established fact, that apart from Nick Berry, everyone in Brighton is a musician of some sort.

Established musos seem to like relocating to Brighton on the grounds that it's close to London and you can wear sunglasses here without fear of being pretentious.

Below is a helpful guide to the pop-stars of past and present who at some time have graced our streets. I must admit though, some of it could be based on hearsay and an over-active imagination.

The very stylish Simon Johns of Stereolab about to give birth to a Mini-Moog

FAMOUS FOR 15 MINUTES

The Piranhas,
Frazier Chorus –
Had a thing about kitchens
Sharkboy
These Animal Men –
NME darlings who lived entirely off
speed and hair dye
Peter And The Test
Tube Babies

FAMOUS NAMES WHO HAVE GRACED OUR TOWN

Kirk Brandon –
Spear Of Destiny
Genesis P Orridge –
Psychic TV and Throbbing Gristle
Kevin Rowland –
Dexy's Midnight Runners
Foz – The Monochrome Set and
David Devant And His Spirit Wife

STILL THROWING TELLIES OUT OF WINDOWS

The Levellers
Fatboyslim
Gaz – Supergrass
David Thomas – Pere Ubu
Adrian – Guitarist from James
Simon Johns – Bassist with
Stereolab, whose favourite all-time
record I happen to know is The Frog
Chorus, but we forgive him

How To Get A Gig In Brighton

OPEN MIC

There are plenty of open mike spots in countless pubs around Brighton that will welcome you with open arms, provided you're not planning on playing 'Stairway to Heaven' on bagpipes. (Actually that appeals in a rather perverse way). Some will be awful and others will be worse but you might just meet some kindred spirits or at least get some free beer for the evening. To find out where they are, find a few of the listings guides in the cafes and newsagents and just go along.

BUT WHAT ABOUT MY BAND?

If you want your band to play here, your best bet will be to try the small venues like The Free Butt and The Lift and any other places you see advertising local bands. Send them a demo, get someone to recommend you or sleep with the promoter.

PROMOTING YOUR GIG

Don't expect to pull a crowd. It is notoriously difficult getting people to come and see you in Brighton when there are so many other potentially better things they could be doing. Stick up a few posters around town but expect to discover the next day that all 500 of them have mysteriously disappeared. Try and bring a few friends instead, using bribery or blackmail. Failing that, get on your knees and weep until at least one of them promises to come. Failing that, ask your parents.

THE SOUNDCHECK

You will be told to arrive at the venue strictly for 6pm, no later. This you do, even though the sound-guy does not show up before 7, and he's had a few already. After the headline band have sound-checked for around 2 hours, you will be given 5 minutes for your sound-check owing to the fact that the doors are about to open. During your sound-check you will notice that the other band will probably giggle at you for a couple of minutes then walk off and ignore you for the rest of the night. Do not be alarmed, this is nothing out of the ordinary. It just means they think you are talentless geeks who are destined to go nowhere fast, unlike them.

Meanwhile on stage you can't hear your vocals at all. When you tell the guy on the mixing desk he will say 'that's as high as I can get'. He is however referring to the cocktail of drugs he took earlier. Beyond this point, he will only hear your voice backwards in his head. As the hallucinations and paranoia kick in, he will stagger out of the venue and never be seen again until the following evening. Your sound-check is now over.

THE PERFORMANCE

You are set to go on stage at 8.40pm but hang on until ten past nine in the hope that there will be more people in the room than the barstaff. The bass player's dad walks in, so on you go. On stage you can hear nothing but feedback and look around for the mixing guy. After 5 minutes he appears momentarily in the room, gives you the thumbs up and disappears again. You frantically wave at him but he's gone. You soldier on.

Where did it all go wrong

AFTER THE GIG

The bass player's dad says 'well done lads'. He tells you that it was a shame the vocals couldn't be heard and asks you nicely what the high pitched whine was throughout the set. Meanwhile the promoter who promised you £20 has gone home and someone's nicked your guitar tuner. The diminutive singer from the other band with eye make-up and a glittery shirt is really pissed now and he comes over to tell you that you were crap before swaggering back to snog his 13-year-old girlfriend.

Well done, you have survived your first gig. Don't be too disheartened though, your ego will be a little bruised but that's all. You have learned a lot and after a bit of a practice you'll soon be ready for your next one.*

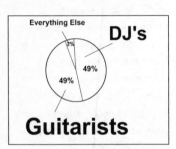

Brighton Musicians Pie Chart

---

* I think it only fair to say that despite my cathartic ramblings, I had a hell of a lot of fun playing in bands over the years.

The Gay Scene

EVER SINCE THE 1900s, Brighton has been home to an ever-expanding gay scene. Secretive at first, but now very much integrated into the town, it has grown to become the UK's most celebrated gay community and second only to London.

The town's theatrical history is deemed to be one of the main factors that helped kick-start the scene, as earlier in the century big gay icons like Ivan Novello and Noel Coward lived here for some time, helping make Brighton a magnet for this secretive and (then) outlawed community. Thanks to this and to Brighton's already well-established reputation as a fashionable pleasure capital, the scene flourished. And of course with places like Dyke Close and signs like 'A friendly welcome greets you in the Queen's Arms', it seemed the obvious choice for the gay community to have its headquarters.

From the 60s onwards, the gay community has developed around Kemptown and the Old Steine. This is where the majority of Brighton's gay population now live and socialise. You will find most of the gay bars, clubs, bookshops and saunas here, especially around St. James's Street.

Many of the gay haunts in Kemptown were developed for cruising, but as it's getting so much easier to be out in Brighton now, in recent years the gay population has been branching into other areas. A small but growing percentage of the gay population is now integrating into the old Brunswick Town area in Hove, which is fast becoming a new gay hot-spot.

There are now believed to be 25,000 gay men and 10-15,000 lesbians living in Brighton, and the scene is growing by over 2000 gay men and women a year.

Where to Hang Out

FASHIONABLE NEW GAY BARS

Amsterdam
11-12 Marine Parade
(01273) 688825

New European-style bar on the seafront, next to the Escape and attracting a large, mixed gay crowd. Arguably an important change in Brighton's gay scene, in that it's very up-front and not just for cruising, but a place to hang out, socialise and be seen.

Although it's a hotel, the sauna and bar are open to the public. Destined to be one of *the* gay haunts.

Coopers Cask
Farm Road, Hove

One of a new breed of gay-run, gay-friendly pubs, with a young, integrated, mixed crowd. Always busy, their policy of table service, sweets at the end of the night and caring staff make them popular among the easy-going gay and straight community. Look out also for their other bars The Druids and The Hop Poles, for more of the same.
(See Pub Section review).

Dr Brighton's
16 Kings Road - (01273) 328765

One of the coolest gay bars in town. This seafront pub is particularly popular at weekends, especially with the pre-club crowd (Revenge, the Zap and The Beach are all within a 5 minutes walk). Athough it is mainly a gay bar, it is straight friendly and very welcoming to lesbians. If you think it looks inviting from the outside, you won't be disappointed when you go in, the atmosphere is always lively and friendly, even though the sign above the bar says 'No Camping'!

LOCAL GAY BARS

The Aquarium
6 Steine Street (01273) 605525

Simple but busy back-street bar with a mixed male orientated gay crowd.

Bedford Tavern
30 Western Street, Hove 739495

Tucked away in Hove, and somewhat off the beaten tracks, this bar has a regular crowd of predominantly older local gay men. The décor leaves a lot to be desired (were brass pistols ever fashionable?) but if you clean out the fish-tank for them, they'll probably make you feel very welcome.

The Bulldog

31 St. James's Street
(01273) 684097

One of the most established gay
bars, in the heart of Kemptown.
The hip and trendy front is slightly
deceiving since this is mostly an
older men's drinking pub.

Queens Head

10 Steine Street (01273) 602939

Recently refurbished traditional gay
pub, frequented by the older gay
community, and a well-known
Brighton landmark for its fabulous
Freddy Mercury pub-sign.

Regency Tavern

32-34 Russell Square (01273)
325652

Indisputably the campest pub in
town, but not wanting to shout
about it. Worth a visit at weekends,
just to see the décor and the
barman's shirt. (See pub reviews)

CABARET & KARAOKE HEAVEN

Black Horse

112 Church Street (01273) 606864

Known affectionately as the Pink
Pony. The place is a regular host
to cabaret and karaoke nights, and
particularly popular with the older
theatre queens. The pool-room is
a well-established butch dykes
hang-out, and the pub is still the
official warm-up bar for the 'Fresh'
crowd on a Friday.

Legends Bar
31-32 Marine Parade
(01273) 624462

Attached to the New Europe Hotel, this place attracts a mature crowd for its regular karaoke and cabaret. On Fridays and Saturdays it's home to the Schwartz bar downstairs, a strictly-leather and uniform bar. If the Village People were in town, they'd drink here.

The Oriental
5 Montpelier Road (01273) 728808

Almost all that's left of the western end of the gay scene since the demise of the Beacon Royal Hotel. This is a popular locals' bar with regular cabaret and karaoke, five nights a week.

Queens Arms
7 George Street
(01273) 696873

Traditional pub with cabaret & karaoke five nights a week. Recently, this entertainment palace has become very popular with women, especially on a Saturday night.

TRANSVESTITE BARS

Ruby's
43 Providence Place
(01273) 620630

Hidden behind Woolworths off the London Road, this is (to my knowledge) the only transvestite-friendly bar in Brighton. Opened by the king of camp, Danny La

Rue, this whole place is a real flashback to the 80s. During the week there is cabaret in the large, glittery bar area upstairs, which sometimes includes some pretty wild drag acts and karaoke. It also attracts quite a few lesbian couples and generally caters for an older crowd, who seem to know each other quite well. Worth a visit, whatever your choice of dress.

CLUBS

Gayte Club
Grand Parade
(01273) 242927

Drinking establishment for gentlemen. The top floor is for food, (American style) and the lower floor for drinking, being social and letting your hair down (if you have any). On sunny days they open up the patio, which has a fabulous view of the Pavilion. Every night is a different theme.

HERBIE

Club Revenge
32-43 Old Steine (01273) 606064

The biggest gay club on the South coast, open six nights a week with special events, drinks promotions and strip-shows. You will find the inevitable cliques,but don't be put off, you should still be able to meet new people. And with all those body beautifuls sweating it out on the upstairs dance-floor, you shouldn't find it hard to get into the contagious party atmosphere. Be nice to the sexy and flirty bar-staff, they are your best port of call to find out everything about the hottest bars and parties in town.

Secrets
5 Steine Street (01273) 609672

Located just behind Scene 22, this place plays a selection of trashy handbag and dance music and attracts a regular young weekend crowd. The club is split into separate levels, so if you don't feel like dancing, then you can hang out upstairs with a less deafening soundtrack.

During the week, it is a popular socialising spot for young and old gay men, and their special evenings include cabaret, and a snakes and ladders night. Is this a new euphemism I haven't come across yet?

Lady Laverne says come and get it duckies!

Zanzibar
129 St. James's Street
(01273) 622100

Small but busy basement club that caters for all age groups. Great place for drinking Monday-Wednesday when its free to get in, with happy hour between 1am-2am. At weekends get there before 10pm or you will find yourself in a queue for a lengthy time. This place is very much like a small London gay club and one of the most popular in Brighton with the younger gay scene.

SPECIAL CLUB NIGHTS

Sunday Sundae
Bar Centro, 2-6 Ship Street
(01273) 206580

Describing itself as 'Brighton's tea dance for gay men and lesbians' this early Sunday club night kicks off at 6pm, playing up-front club anthems and classic disco, and is hosted by the very lovely Miss Marilyn.

*See club section for reviews of the
Pussycat Club at the Zap, Wild Fruit
at the Paradox, and Vavavavoom! at
the Gloucester.*

Drag Queens

Brighton's most glamorous drag-
queen Lady Laverne recommends
that the best places to show off
your new frock and high heels are
still The Pussycat Club at The Zap
(on a Friday), Vavavoom!, Revenge,
and of course Wild Fruit.

CAFES

Scene 22

St. James's Street (01273) 626682

Scene 22 is a popular first stop
for gays and lesbians coming to
Brighton, and its owner Freddie is
a real charmer, who seems to
have endless time for anyone that

drops in. It's amusing just to listen
to the banter between him and
the regular customers, as the
saucy double-entendres flow
thick and fast. There you go, I'm
at it now.

Scene 22 is also a good place
to find information on health
matters and pick up free maps and
magazines. You can even make
hotel bookings, collect tickets for
shows, and leave messages on the
notice board for anything (or
anyone) you fancy.

Don't forget to have a nose
around the shop in the back, it
sells your usual toys, lubes,
vibrators and other goodies, and
don't be surprised if Freddie
manages to persuade you into
buying a kit to make your cock ten
times bigger. It's his way of saying
that he likes you.

BRIGHTONS ONLY GAY SHOP & COFFEE BAR
129 ST James Street, Brighton. Telephone: 01273 626682

CRUISING AREAS

Duke's Mound
Located 10 mins walk east of the pier, overlooking the nudist beach

This area in Brighton is essentially a small hillside of bushes on the seafront, which has become an integral part of the cruising scene. It offers enough privacy for those needing it, yet is risqué enough for you naughty exhibitionists. Rumour has it that they are starting to do some work around there soon and it is likely that the cruisers will find themselves coming more towards Hove lawns. While it isn't that commonly reported, there are occasional stories of people getting mugged, robbed etc after being picked up and taken to Dukes Mound, so be careful.

Nudist Beach
Located about 10 min East of the Palace Pier

Brighton's nudist beach is primarily a gay haunt. Straights are welcome but in most cases will feel slightly uneasy. There is a lot of parading, the occasional erection and plenty of voyeurs.

Hove Lawns
Starting at Brunswick Square on the seafront

Increasingly popular cruising area for gay men, especially on Sunday

evenings. It's a lot more open here than Duke's Mound and is a nice place to hang out, especially with The Meeting House café nearby.

SAUNAS

Used as social clubs in Brighton by the gay community, the saunas attract a wide age group and all come with rest room facilities.

Denmark Oasis
75-76 Grand Parade
(01273) 689966

Opposite the Pavilion and done out in a glorious Egyptian theme, this is one of the newest and nicest of the saunas in Brighton.

There is a whirlpool, steam room, sun beds, coffee shops, and qualified masseurs. During the week it is £11 to get in, although at the weekend it is only £7 and that includes in and out privileges for the day (!!!)

UNDERSTANDING THE LINGO

Chicken
Dictionary says – on the look-out for new boys fresh to the area.

Eg Check out the chicken outside The Fortune of War on a hot sunny afternoon.

Trade
Dictionary says – Your pick-up for the evening.

Eg Take your trade home and give him something to remember you by.

Varda
Dictionary says – To check out.
Eg Varda the legs on him.

Cruising
Dictionary says – Sail to and fro for protection of shipping, making for no particular place or calling at a series of places.

Hmmm, that just doesn't seem to be what's going on in the bushes.

HANKY PANKY

Developed in the days when secrecy was necessary, the coloured hankie in the back pocket is still used in some bars for gay men to express their sexual preferences.

Yellow Hankie
Into water-sports

Red Hankie
Into fist fucking*

Green Hankie
Into the washing-machine it goes for a good clean

*In the left back-pocket means you like taking, right back-pocket means you like giving. Or was it the other way around? Oh well, you'll find out one way or another.

Amsterdam Hotel
11-12 Marine Parade
(01273) 688825

New sauna offering steamroom, showers and darkroom. This is open to the public and at £5 a time, it seems remarkably good value for money. Open from 6pm all night, but there are plans for them soon to be going round the clock.

Unit One
St. Margarets High Street,
Rottingdean (01273) 307253

THE LESBIAN SCENE

For years the lesbian scene in Brighton has almost been non-existent, which is strange, considering the large numbers who live here. Although in principle most of the gay bars welcome lesbians, few venture in. Recently however, a social scene for gay women has finally started to develop in Brighton. The first lesbian-run pub, The Marlborough, has been running for two years now, and with several club-nights growing ever-popular things seem at last to be changing.

BARS/CLUB NIGHTS

Marlborough
4 Princes Street (01273) 570028

Tucked away behind the Old Steine, this is Brighton's main lesbian-friendly bar. Well known for its little theatre upstairs, the pub still puts on plays, comedy nights and other events, especially during the festival, and is a good place to pick up gay magazines and information.

There are two bars, a lively one with a pool table and a quieter one at the back. Popular nights are Tuesdays and Thursdays for students, and at the weekend the bar gets very busy with mixed crowds and guest DJs. Known to be one of Brighton's most haunted pubs, the ghost of Lucy Packham occasionally pops her head round for a quick game of pool.

Cowlick
The Sanctuary, 51-55 Brunswick Street East (01273) 770002
Opens 7.30pm

Downstairs at the Sanctuary, this lesbian social hangout has been running for over two years now and has special mike nights and different performances each week.

Fresh
Friday nights at the
Royal Pavilion Tavern
Castle Square (01273) 827641

Still one of the most popular lesbian nights in Brighton, catering for all ages, and attracting a young dressy crowd who have a reputation for knowing how to knock back the booze!

Just Sisters Night
At the Aida Pub on
the Kingsway, Hove

Popular lesbian night held once a

month in this Hove bar, hidden away on the seafront.

Shebeen

At the Hanbury Arms, 83 St. George's Road (01273) 605789 For dates and details call (01273) 738712 / 327442

Women-only night *'appealing to sassy, classy gals'* every Wednesday, 8pm-late.

The flavour of this successful night seems to change every month, including pop-quizzes, performances, birthday parties, singing, poetry and erotic dancing. It's even known to have the occasional appearance by the only out-lesbian belly dancer in the UK.

SUPPORT GROUPS

Brighton's Woman's Centre

Lettice House, 10 St. Georges Mews, off Trafalgar Street (01273) 600526 www.btnwomen.u-net.com

Offering supportive help and information in a friendly atmosphere. Their services range from accommodation boards, use of photocopier and computer to free pregnancy tests, creche, counselling and legal advice.

SPECIAL EVENTS

Gay Pride

August 14th Preston Park Starts at 1pm

Gay Pride was attended by just 100 people when it first started, and has now expanded to be one of the biggest highlights in Brighton's calendar. Gay and straight men and women from all over the country turn up for this annual bash. There are floats, bands, costumes, cabaret, stalls and shows, and it's fantastic, so don't miss it. The march usually starts at 1pm from the peace statue, and dances, shouts and parades its way to the Park, stopping only for a sandwich and glass of fizzy pop at the Woolworths café on the way.

Ms Brighton Alternative

Usually held in August

Another un-missable day in Brighton's gay calendar. Different performers, loads of false boobies, never enough make-up and only one winner. Check local press while you're here, to see if it's on though, as endless nonsense recently has jeopardised it taking place.

IMPORTANT INFORMATION

Safe sex?

Condoms are given free almost everywhere in Brighton, yet still they don't appear to get used. Don't bury your head in the sand, the HIV and AIDS numbers are well on the increase again here, yet 'it wont happen to me' is all some guys seem to be thinking. Thankfully most gay prostitutes in Brighton do enforce the condom rule. Just remember, sex is as safe as you're prepared to make it, so wrap up your peckers guys.

Problems Against Gays Here?

The gay scene is a big part of the town's life, and most people in Brighton are totally cool and supportive of the gay community. Like anywhere however, a certain amount of bigotry and homophobia exists.

There are known to be occasional reports of violence against gays and although it isn't rampant, one attack is one too many. Try and avoid snogging in the middle of West Street at 2am in the morning, and you should be OK.

BOOKSHOPS & MAGAZINES

OUT!

Dorset Street
Open Mon-Thu 10am-6pm
Fri-Sat 10am-7pm, Sun 11am-5pm

One of only three UK gay bookshops, with stock ranging from dyke detective stories to queer history. If you're after magazines, critical theory or fiction it's definitely worth seeking out.

G-Scene Magazine

Your gay and lesbian bible for your visit here, (along with *The Cheeky Guide*, of course) with previews of all the special club nights, and up-to-date information, from health and community issues, to restaurant reviews and personal ads. And amazingly, it's free.

SUPPORT NUMBERS

Brighton Lesbian And Gay Switchboard
(01273) 204050

Support and information for lesbians and gay men between 6pm-11pm nightly.

Brighton Lesbian / Gay Community Centre
(01273) 234005

Information centre and informal support on lesbian and gay issues. Mon-Fri 10am-12noon. Drop in Thursday 12noon-4pm, women only on Friday 12noon-4pm

Brash
(01273) 293632 or (0973 873715)
Group meetings for young gay and bisexual men.

Brighton Relate
(01273) 697997
Specialist advice for lesbian and gay relationships.

HIV Related Support Open Door
(01273) 605706
Support, referrals, advice, meals, therapies for HIV.
Mon-Fri 10am-4pm.

Brighton and Hove HIV Project Bureau
(01273) 327474
Employment, benefits, money and housing information. By appointment only Tuesday and Thursday 9am-4pm, Wednesday 9am-12.30pm.

Brighton Body Positive
(01273) 693266
Complimentary therapies, information, support, and counselling for HIV /AIDS

Gay Men's Health Matters
(01273) 625222
Information about HIV and sexual health, free condoms given.

Street Outreach Service (SOS)
(01273) 625577

Mobile AIDS prevention unit, lots of advice and free condoms and lube.

Claude Nicol Centre
(01273) 664721
Testing and treatment for HIV (Same day results on Mon-Tue) free and confidential service.

Wilde Clinic
(01273) 664722
Gay and Bisexual men's health clinic, does HIV testing, STI testing and treatment, hepatitis A & B Vaccinations.

GAY HOTELS

Roland House
(01273) 603693

Catnaps
(01273) 685193

Hudsons
(01273) 683642

New Europe
(01273) 624462

Shalimar
(01273) 605316

Amsterdam
(01273) 688825

Sex & Fetish

Traditionally Brighton has always been the place where fat London bosses with hairy bums bring their secretaries for more than just a tele-sales conference. Being a fashionable resort, and the perfect short break from the Big Smoke, is probably why Brighton earned its reputation for 'dirty weekends' and countless indiscretions. Even the Prince Regent was at it, having secretly married Mrs Fitzherbert here. The passageways connecting the Pavilion bedroom to her place were a means of assuring their midnight rendezvous were kept a secret.

Brighton's saucy reputation today comes more from the liberal nature of its citizens than anything else. It's a good place to live for anyone who wants to come out of the closet and feel relaxed with their sexuality. From fetishists to drag queens, you can feel comfortable in the knowledge that in this town there'll always be someone kinkier than you.

WHAT'S ON?

Kentucky Woman

Provide information for any local and London fetish events. They also organise their own discrete fetish evenings occasionally.

Scene 22

Stock all the information you need for gay club nights like Wild Fruit, and other related information.

Wildcats

Usually have fliers for things like The Sexual Freedom Coalition parties and fetish events in London and Brighton.

SHOPPING

Angel

29 Sydney St (01273) 623839
Open Mon-Sat 11-6pm

Selection of unusual platform and fetish boots together with good quality PVC clothing at reasonable prices. You can also find the occasional rubber bargain too. Downstairs is a popular piercing studio and tattoo studio. (See Tattoo Section)

Ann Summers
The top of North Street, opposite the Clock Tower

Banana dick lip, after dinner nipples, beginners SM kits, willy wash, maids outfits, sexy lingerie, cheap rubber and PVC, dildos and naughty books. It's sex with a smile and a perfect starting point if you're here for a saucy weekend. The clothes are hardly top notch but then you won't necessarily be wearing them out, will you?

EU Videos
21 Preston Street
Open Mon-Sat 12noon-10pm
Adults only

Stockists of gay and straight videos, most of which you just read about in their catalogues then buy over the counter. And they're only £10 each. Not bad for a quiet night in.

Kentucky Woman
19 George Street (01273) 601961
www.kentuckywoman.co.uk
Open Mon-Sat 10.30am-6pm

If you're new to the fetish scene, this shop will make you feel totally at ease. Stockists of a wide range of PVC, rubber and leather clothes and fetish accessories, including clothes for cross dressers. They also do made-to-measure clothes

BEST 69 POSITION LOVLIEST SWEDISH
COME LICK MY MELON'S
* OUTCALLS WELCOME * VIP TREATMENT

and mail order. There's even a fully equipped dungeon in the basement you can hire out during the day at £50 a shot, morning or afternoon. Evenings are out though as part owner John gets fetish fatigue by then and starts fantasising about working in a bank. This is a service strictly for couples, voyeurs will not be welcome. Very friendly, treating fetish as fun not seedy.

Private Shop
11 Surrey Street
Open Mon-Sat 9am-5.30pm
Adults only

The usual collection of dildos, magazines, videos, blow-up dolls and mild fetish toys and clothes. They do seem to have a good selection of foot fetish magazines. Did I really see a whole collection of mud-wrestling videos there?

PUSSYCATS

**THE BEST & ONLY
LAPDANCING CLUB
IN SUSSEX**

Topless Tabledancing

Stage Cabaret

Open 5pm - Late

Group Bookings Welcome

Discreet Receipts

Corporate / VIP Lounge

Video's & DVD's Available

**Two Girl
Lapdancing Our Speciality**

**The Basement, 176 Church Road, Hove
Bookings - (01273) 709100 or Club (01273) 735574
Email - sales@pussycatclub.co.uk**
Browse our spectacular website

www.pussycatclub.co.uk

**free entry and membership if you bring your
cheeky guide with you and show us this advert**

Wildcats
16 Preston Street (01273) 323758
Open Mon-Sat 10am-6pm
Strictly for the over 18s

Not only the largest suppliers of body jewellery in the world but also stockists of tattoo books, fetish mags and some toys for the more adventurous.

LAPDANCING CLUBS

Pussycat Club
The Basement, 176 Church Road, Hove (01273) 735574
£10 compulsory membership
Mon-Thur £5 Weekends £10
Lap-dance £10 Free entry and membership on presentation of your 'Cheeky Guide'

If your idea of fun is having a beautiful girl rubbing her voluptuous breasts in front of you then you may want to pay this place a visit.* The club attracts stag nights, rugby teams and visiting businessmen. There's a friendly feel to the place and everyone seems genuinely eager to please.

Shy voyeurs, be warned, it's quite small down there and not the sort of place you can hide yourself away in. Jeremy had to go down once to chat to the owner about advertising, but auditions were going on all afternoon, so he ended up being the judge. When one of the women said she'd been quite nervous Jeremy unwittingly said – 'it was just as hard for me.'

PROSTITUTION

You'll find a variety of cards and phone numbers in the phone boxes around the Old Steine and Western Road areas. £40 for 30 minutes is a typical price to pay but if you shop around, you might get a student discount. Typically, new laws are being pushed through to stamp out the card system here, which will probably push prostitution back onto the street. There are also numerous brothels around town but we couldn't possibly tell you where they are – sorry.

---

*If you don't know the law, you can pay for a personalised topless dance, but no physical contact is allowed.

SAUNAS

Ambassador's Sauna & Massage

37 Portland Road, Hove
0870 7409439 Open
12noon-10pm Basic cost £20

This highly rated five-star sauna with a jacuzzi offers a full range of services, including more unusual massages, and photographic portfolios of all the members of staff in various costumes (such as Tarzan's Jane and Miss Santa). Private parties can be catered for, and in summer there's even an outdoor massage facility.

Like Sainsbury's, they have a reward card system, save enough points and you can have a free two-girl Swedish massage or a digital watch.

Top To Toe

37 Lower Market Street
0870 740 9442
Open 10am-10pm Basic cost £30

Another five-star sauna boasting a sauna, jacuzzi, uniforms and videos. An international range of lovely ladies await, to tickle your fancy with a sensuous massage.

TATTOOISTS & PIERCERS

In the last few years, Brighton has seen a real boom in tattoo parlours and body piercing studios. The following are only a local selection, but they are the ones I would recommend because either I have been there myself or close friends have had stuff done here.

Although tattooing is probably a universal skill, please bear in mind that design and style taste are very individual. So if you're thinking of getting one, I'd recommend that you make an appointment with some of the guys and girls that follow. Go in person to see if you feel comfortable with them, and what you think of their work. All good tattooists should carry a portfolio.

Stigmata

29 Sydney Street (01273) 686369
Appointments only

All tattoos here are custom-designed. The idea behind this being that a tattoo should be as individual as the person who wears it.

They specialise in black tattoos, with a lot of influence drawn from Maori, Celtic, Haida and Art Nouveau. Don't go in with a tribal drawing and expect to get an exact copy. Tattooist Sophie (one of the resident artists) believes each tribal tattoo has an intrinsic meaning, which should not be plagiarised outright from its original culture. Her motto is – 'A tattoo should look like it's evolved and grown out of the body's line.' They also do grey shading and cover-up. In short, anything beautiful.

Wizard Of Ink

74 North Road (01273) 626199
Mobile 0410 471289
Open Mon-Fri 11am-5pm
Sat 10am-6pm Walk in only

Flash and custom work. This place is probably of the more conventional, no-nonsense, walk in, pick a design off the wall and get-it-done type of parlour. If you're into the philosophical side of tattooing, this place isn't for you. They also have three piercers working full-time (including a girl for the more coy ladies) who will pierce anything above the waist.

Temple Tatu

9 Boyces Street (01273) 208844

This impressive tattoo studio is located just off the busy Duke's Lane. Although they do walk-ins, appointments are encouraged in order to give people the chance to really look into their motivations for getting a tattoo. The three resident artists have a deep knowledge and understanding of the history of tattooing and make each design individual and unique.

Newcomers are made to feel at ease by discussing over a cup of tea all that the process will involve in the beautiful surroundings. In fact, the reception room at Temple Tatu probably contributes a lot to inspiring you with confidence in these guys' creative

The Glitzy Tartz crew get a few discrete tattoos

skills. From hand-made sequin tiaras to Hindu tiles and stickers, this place has been decorated to welcome you in and make you feel at home.

While here look out for the two kitsch-looking alchemical shrines built by some mad-genius New Zealander, with plastic dolls, driftwood, electric bulbs and old soap boxes inside. You can activate one of them by inserting a coin and pressing your palms on the designated space. Loads of weird shit happens, including stuff whizzing around and the thing talking to you and playing strange music. The shrine is designed to release positive energy, and frankly with the effort and esoteric detail that has gone into these things, I'd happily have one in my lounge if I could afford it.

I can't really tell you what they specialise in, since their portfolio is so varied (black, tribal, colour, cover up). However, they're quite particular about researching every design, so that you can find out what the tattoo you're about to get really means.

Perforations

21 Preston Street (01273) 743723
www.perforations.com
email: piercing@perforations.com

A state-of-the-art studio where piercings are more than just skin-deep. Check their website, it's really informative.

Penetration

29 Sydney Street (01273) 623839
Open Mon-Sat 10.30am-6pm

Piercings here are a totally different experience. While he pierces your tongue, Martin (patron and resident piercer) will tell you all about when he got his willy pierced for the benefit of an Italian TV fashion programme, to which The Pope didn't bat an eyelid.

They totally look after their 'patients' here, to the point that if you're a fainter you get given sweeties. For the more hard-core body-modifications addict, apart from the usual PA and ampallangs (for which you need a consultation to get you…ahem…measured), they also do surgical steel implants and cosmetic dentistry.

A Temple Tatu design

Brighton

in Books

& Movies

Brighton Rock
1947 Dir. John Boulting

Discover a Brighton of Bovril
adverts and bryl cream. This classic
Grahame Greene story set in the
30s has plenty of scenes from the
Old Lanes, Queens Road and the
West Pier. Richard Attenborough
plays Pinkie Brown, an evil small-
time gangster who tries to cover
up a murder by marrying a young
girl who could give evidence
against him. The ending is better in
the book (aren't they always) but
it's a genuinely chilling account of
the gangster scene that used to
flourish here. Doctor Who fans
should look out for William
Hartnell.

Classic line from the film:

*'People don't change, look at me.
I'm like one of those sticks of rock.
Bite all the way down and you still
read Brighton.'*

Quadrophenia
1979 Dir. Franc Roddam

Welcome to the Brighton of
Triumph Heralds and Wimpy bars.

A troubled young mod visits
Brighton with his mates for a
shandy and a scrap but gets
carried away. You know the story.
The fighting scenes take place on
the beach and down East Street in
front of the blue pub on the
corner (The New Heart and
Hand), which is now The Prodigal.

To find the famous alleyway
where Jimmy and Steph had sex,
go down East Street towards the
sea, and near the end look for the
shop LTS and a sign for an alleyway
that reads *'to little East Street'*. It's
down there. Once a graffitied
shrine to the movie, all that seems
to have gone now, and the next
Mod revival is not due for another
10 years. Yes, the doorway is still

there (now black) but it's locked, so no, you can't pop in and have a shag. Imagine how many people have tried though.

Classic line from the film:
'I don't want to be like everyone else, that's why I'm a Mod see.'

Villain
1971 Dir. Michael Tuchner

This Richard Burton movie from the 70s is a tough bruising thriller with Burton playing a vicious gay criminal. Set in London, he does however find his way to Brighton to visit his dear old mother. But the game is eventually up when he gets nabbed by the fuzz on the West Pier.

The Slade classic FLAME
1975 Dir. Richad Loncraine

Thanks to Ian for mentioning this particular gem to me. The plot charts the rise of Midland pub band Flame (played by the Brummie boys) who eventually become glam superstars. Of course it all goes awry after one too many babyshams on tour and ends with a brawl in The famous Grand Hotel. Look out for Tom Conte as the manager.

The Fruit Machine
1988 Dir. Philip Saville

Gay drama set around the seedier tourist areas in Brighton. Shots of West Street, the amusement arcades and the Escape club.

CARRY ON BRIGHTON

Carry On Girls
1973 Dir. Gerald Thomas

The Plot:
'Sid James is on the make as usual, this time as the buttock-slapping Councilor Fiddler who organises a beauty competition, only to be foiled by the sour-faced women's-libber June Whitfield.'

Where In Brighton?:
It all takes place in the pretend seaside town of Fircombe (oooerrr!!) which is in fact Brighton. The film features shots of the seafront, the West Pier and a fleeting glimpse of Regency Square.

My favourite bit of the film is near the end, when the contest goes awry and Sid James escapes down the West Pier in a go-kart whilst being chased by a crowd of angry men.

Trivia:

This was the first Carry On film that had to go after the 9pm BBC watershed, as it was considered too saucy.

Carry On At Your Convenience
1971 Dir. Gerald Thomas

The Plot:

'Industrial strife at WC Boggs lavatory factory gives ample opportunity for some toilet humour. '

With Kenneth Williams as WC Boggs and Sid James as…Sid. Well, why make life difficult?

Where In Brighton?:

The workers have a day trip out in Brighton and visit the usual haunts down on the seafront and along the Palace Pier.

Trivia:

Alternative title for the film Carry On Ladies Please Be Seated.

Brighton
and the
Written Word

BRIGHTON TALES

Beatniks
Toby Litt

Tale of three modern day hippies who move to Brighton to start a magazine called 'Café Bohemia' but all end up in bed together instead. The book tries hard (but fails) to be hip, and the descriptions of Brighton are all a bit cliched. Strangely enough, there is a Café Bohemia in Kemptown, which opened up just as the book was released. Coincidence or synchronicity? All I know is that it is perhaps the least bohemian café I've ever been in.

Breakfast In Brighton
Nigel Richardson

A subtle blend of fact and fiction makes up this excellent story. The author takes you on a personal journey through the many faces of Brighton, with some wild descriptions of its renegade characters, from drunkards to actors.

Hangover Square
Patrick Hamilton

Companion to 'Brighton Rock', detailing the sleaze and vitality of London and Brighton of the late 30s.

As Good As It Gets
Simon Nolan

Trendy novel about a bunch of twenty-somethings who find 5 kilos of coke and decide that they could find a better use for it than the police. Good descriptions of the pub and club culture in Brighton and some funny moments. Think Irvine Welsh on Prozac.

Brighton Rock
Graham Greene

See film guide.

Queenspark Books

This local publishing company put out a range of books on the theme of local people's stories. Such gems include:

Moulsecoomb Memoirs

Tales from the Fishing Community

BRIGHTON AUTHORS

Keith Waterhouse
Billy Liar
Jeffrey Bernard Is Unwell

Jack Sargent
Deathtripping
(Cinema Of Transgression)

Helen Zahave
Dirty Weekend

Suzannah Dunn
Tenterhooks

Bertie Marshall
Queercore Literature

Jay Merrick
Horse Latitude

If you want to know more about the literary side of Brighton, talk to the guys in Waterstones. They really know their stuff.

LITERARY EVENTS
Do Tongues

Brighton's longest established spoken word pioneers, who over the years have put on some remarkable performances by the likes of Ken Campbell, Jah Wobble, Jeff Noon and Will Self. I think one of my favourite memories of Do Tongues was seeing a guy called Jim Dodge from the States who entertained about 10 of us upstairs in the Mash Tun one night with a story about his dog getting its testicles stuck in the bathtub. It was one of those priceless evenings where you wouldn't be anywhere else for the world. Will it be running for another year? I don't know, look out for the posters or ask Annie in Waterstones, she's always clued up on these kinds of things.

Both Waterstones and Borders also regularly put on spoken word evenings as does the Komedia and the Tamarind Tree. (See Restaurant Section)

Adventures With Brighton's Most Eccentric Shopkeeper

FORNICATING BABOONS

— Hello, can I help you Sir?

— I'm just browsing thanks.

I start to weave my way around the bundles of suits hanging up in the shop.

The shopkeeper follows close on my heels:

— Tell me Sir, why ARE the South Downs so cold?

— I beg your pardon?

— The South Downs Sir, why are they so cold?

— Er, well I don't know, I'm not a geography teacher.

— Aren't you Sir? May I ask what you are Sir?

— Well I…. I sometimes teach music.

— Do you Sir? Would you like to come upstairs and play my piano?

— Pardon?

— My piano Sir, it's upstairs. Would you care to play for me?

I find myself saying 'yes, alright' and follow him upstairs into a room that is inconceivibly packed with clothes and junk. In the corner there appear to be the remains of a piano, covered in dust and a whole array of paraphenalia. I take a heroic leap across the room and land near it. Getting the lid open is tricky owing to all the heavy objects on it. I get it half open and play a couple of notes. It is appallingly out of tune and I tell him. He does not appear to be listening, but instead is talking to a rack of ties in the corner of the room. He sees I have finished and says

— Perhaps Sir would like to come back and have piano lessons here?

I mutter something vaguely negative, but he continues unabated.

*— My uncle Sir, was a famous
violinist. Played to millions.
Mantovani personally approved of
him. Of course he's dead now.
Buried underground. You could dig
him up if you wanted to. But that
wouldn't prove that he really played
the violin though, would it?*

**We move downstairs. At the
bottom of the stairs he bends
over to pick something up
from behind a dense pile of
suits. It's a book of English
Politics from the 1960s. He
opens it up and inside is his
name and the year 1968.**

*— I'd like to go back to school Sir. I
left when I was only 15, but I did
win a prize once.*

**I presume it's the book. It
isn't. The reason for him
bringing out the book in the
first place is never made clear.**

*— We could have any book we
wanted so I asked for The Human
Zoo by Desmond Morris. Do you
know him Sir?*

I nod.

*— But the headmistress wouldn't
allow it Sir, all those fornicating
animals. Not Homo Sapiens, but
animals Sir. We are Homo Sapiens
aren't we Sir?*

What did that mean?? I nod.

*— Of course I was nearly old
enough to be a father Sir, but not
old enough to look at pictures of*

fornicating baboons.

— Pardon?

*— Would you like to buy this book
Sir?*

**He motions to the book in
his hand.**

— Isn't it special to you?

*— No Sir, I've already read it. But I
don't think that you could afford it Sir.*

**A customer has been standing
by the door now for 5
minutes.**

**I point this out to him. He
doesn't look around but asks**

*— What is your definition of a
customer Sir?*

**He moves away and faces the
customer. It's an old guy with
a jacket in his hand. He
speaks slowly.**

*— I bought this jacket from you and
I'm happy with it but one of the
buttons has come off.*

*— Well you can't be that happy
with it can you Sir? – He says
nastily.*

*— I just want the button replaced.
Have you got a button box?*

— I'm sorry Sir, I don't understand.

— A button box.

— A button box Sir?

— Yes, a box with spare buttons in it.

*— I'm sorry, I really don't
understand. What is Sir's definition
of a button?...*

SOME VELVET MORNING

— Hello, can I help you Sir?

— Well I'm looking for a…

— Certainly Sir.

And he leads me around the labyrinth, offering here a tweed overcoat, there cavalry pantaloons. Eventually I put my foot down and force the issue.

— Actually I'm looking for a double— breasted velvet suit.

The world falls from around us and a heavy feeling hangs in the air.

— Velvet?

— Yes that's right – I say somewhat cautiously – Black and double breasted.

— But……..velvet? – Again the question comes.

— Yes, but if you don't stock velvet I'll……

— Am I right in assuming Sir wants a suit? A man's suit? Made from, what was it, 'velvet'?

— Yes.

And suddenly noticing the very thing not a step away I pronounce –

— Like that one.

But its too late.

— In all my years in the business, I've never heard of anything like it – he says incredulously.

— A suit. A mans suit!

MADE OF VELVET!!

I decide to cut my losses and ask for any suit, just to end the spiral of recriminations against velvet. The storm breaks.

— Of course Sir! I've just the thing.

And with that he brandishes forth the crumbling apparel of Napoleon. The thing has epaulets, gold braid and jodhpurs!

As I'm hurriedly leaving I hear him say –

— Of course it is a little generous in the waist, but we could pad it out with citrus fruit no doubt……

Useful Information

Tourist Information

10 Batholomew Square
(01273) 292599
Open Mon-Fri 9am-5pm
Sat 10am-5pm Sun 10am-4pm
Order an accommodation guide
on 0345 573512
Map of Brighton by fax
+44 0839 401259

Located near the sea front, close to
the bus depot and behind The
Thistle Hotel. By a strange twist of
fate most of the staff here are ex-
circus performers. Ask them about
their days in the big top and they'll
be happy to share a few stories. If
it's information you're after they can
also sort out on-the-day bookings
for B&Bs and hotels, as well as for
National Express coaches and day
trips. You'll also find all the usual
gubbins about local tours, museums
and places to visit here.

HOSPITALS

Brighton General
Elm Grove, Brighton (01273) 696 011

New Sussex Hospital
Brighton (01273) 725351

Royal Sussex County
Eastern Road
(01273) 696 55

Nuffield
55 New Church Road, Hove
(01273) 779471

Southlands
Upper Shoreham Road Shoreham
(01273) 455622

Family Planning
Morning after pill etc
(01273) 242091

LATE NIGHT CHEMISTS

BRIGHTON

Ashtons
98 Dyke Road Seven Dials 9am-
10pm (01273) 325020

Westons Coombe
6 Terrace 9am-10pm
(01273) 605354

Stallions
5 Lewes Road Until 6.45pm
(01273) 604576

Moss Chemists
(Asda, Brighton Marina) Until 8pm
(01273) 688019

Sharps Pharmacy
26 Coombe Road 9am-7pm
(01273) 604384

M.J Stallion
94 Preston Drove Until 6.30pm
(01273) 552808

Sainsburys
Lewes Road 8.30am-8pm
(01273) 674201

HOVE

Codex Chemist
314 Portland Road Until 6.30pm
(01273) 418129

Kamsons
4 Parade Hangleton Until 6.30pm
(01273) 733718

Co-op
Neville Road Until 8pm

POLICE

Central Brighton
(01273) 606744

Hove
(01273) 778922

Shoreham
(01273) 440055

Lewes
(01273) 475432

OTHER INFORMATION

Citizens Advice
(01273) 772277

Brighton And Hove Council
(01273) 290000

Latest Postal Collection
North Road Sorting Office has a late collection at 8pm.

Crime

The usual stuff about being vigilant for pickpockets applies here as anywhere really. I don't have much extra advice on this except that if you hang around on West Street at the weekend for long enough, you will probably end up in a fight.

Drugs

Drugs advice and Information service (01273) 321000

Because drug-use is widespread in Brighton, the clubs are very strict with their policies. You will see countless clubs whose advertising features PVC-clad models smoking huge reefers and the club night is called 'Dope-tastic!' or something. The reality is that all they really want to do is sell you expensive gassy lager. One whiff of grass and you'll be chucked out, as a friend of mine recently discovered. If you want to purchase legal highs check out the review for Hocus Pocus.

INTERNET @CCESS

Need to find a web-site for the best donkey-ride in Brighton or maybe your mum needs to e-mail you some clean socks? Here's where it all happens.

Vyrus Game Zone

(aka The Arena) 36 Preston Road
(01273) 245105
Open daily 12noon-10pm

At time of going to press there were divorce proceedings going on with the owners and an identity crisis with the name, but I am assured that business will be as normal.

Prices are charged by the minute, so cheap access here

H And C

109 Western Road
(01273) 772882
20% off internet price if you show up with this book but not during happy hour)
15 min for £1.95, 30 min for £2.95 or an hour for £ 4.95

This is a small computer shop along Western Road, with the

upstairs converted for internet access. Happy hour is between 5pm and 6pm weekdays (£1 per hour for internet access) and you get a free coffee and Scooby snacks.

Sumo Bar
Middle Street
01273 823344
Internet access
costs £3 per 30 min

Stylish café built on the ashes of The Cybar.* When I last went here all the computers were floating around in the basement as they had just had a flood downstairs, but I'm sure they'll have dried out on the radiators by now.

Brighton Media Centre
Middle Street
(01273) 384200

Check your e-mail here if you need to, it's close to the hostels on middle street and close to the seafront.

Mailboxes Etc
91 Western Road (01273) 786020
15 min £2, 30 min £2.90
and 1 hour for £ 4.70

This is one of those franchises that you see in every town. The prices are reasonable but it isn't the coolest place to go surfing. And that's what matters.

---

*Brighton's first internet café, the Cybar, folded in 1998 when the ZX81 bars started to become fashionable in the North Laines.

Outside Brighton

BEACHY HEAD

Celebrated suicide spot, which featured in Quadrophenia and several Python sketches. It gets pretty windy up there so be careful near the edge but if you're feeling brave look for the spooky old burned-out car half way down the cliffs, I think it's still there. It takes about forty-five minutes to reach here from Brighton and there's not much else around but it's definitely worth a visit, especially for or if your morbid curiosity is aroused or you're a die-hard Mod.

LEWES

Generally speaking this is a cosy little town where you could take your parents for the afternoon (and I have) for a stroll round the castle and a sniff through some old bookshops. It is most notorious however for being host to the largest fireworks event in the UK (see diary of events). Below the surface the town has more than its share of occultists and witches but whether you get any feel of this from an afternoon visit is another matter.
(15 minutes drive from Brighton).

Stanmer Park

Go out of Brighton on the A27 towards Lewes and you'll find it just before Sussex University. There's ample room for big footie games and Frisbee throwing, or you could go lose yourselves in the woods for a bit of nooky. There's an organic farm and the usual teashop, which is next to a stable full of cows, and always smells of shit. But we love it because it's good old-fashioned country shit. It's the closest place to Brighton I know where you can forget the crowds, especially if you take the walk past the village and up the hill. Look out for the tree trunk carved into animals.
10 minutes drive from Brighton.

DEVIL'S DYKE

So the story goes that the devil started to dig a deep chasm here to let the sea in to drown all the pious villagers of the Weald. But an old lady on hearing the noise, lit a candle and tricked the devil into believing it to be the rising sun. So the devil left his terrible work unfinished- a 300ft valley in the heart of the Downs.

Now I know there are several flaws in this local myth (like why didn't the devil come back the next night) but we'll let it pass as it's a good story. This is a popular beauty spot with plenty of walks. There's a good one down the hill to the pub in Fulkin if you can face the journey back again. Expect crowds at the weekend. The Dyke is a twenty-minute drive out of Brighton and in summer you can usually catch an open top bus there.

DITCHLING

It's your typically nice country village with an amazing cake shop (huge treacle tarts for about a quid). Beyond the pond there's a walk I really like because you get a great view of The Downs. To find where it starts, look for the sign that says-

'Public right of way, except for 21st December when for legal reasons this is not open to the public.' (I'd love to know why)

Go up the hill, take a picnic and enjoy the view. Expect to share the field with a few friendly cows.

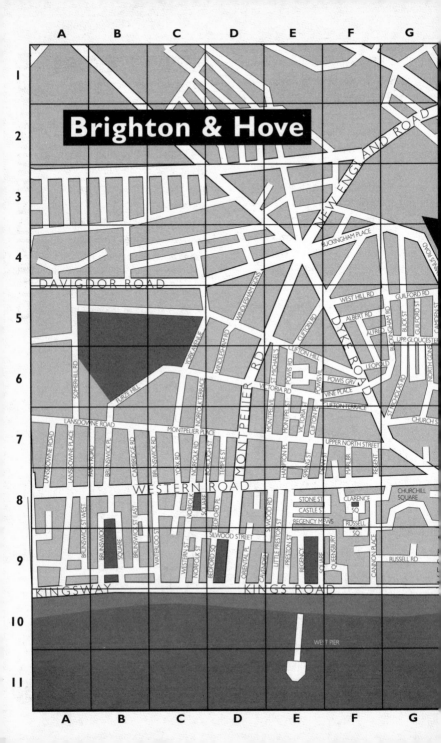

INDEX OF STREETS

Notes:

Build a new golf-course and within a year someone will turn it into an outdoor venue with live DJs, and half the town standing around the holes using them as ashtrays. You cannot keep the party spirit down.

There is a well known story that Elton John came here in the late 80s and tried to buy the Royal Pavilion as somewhere to store his colossal wardrobe and sunglasses.

Typically the townsfolk reacted by forming a huge ring arounds the building and blowing raspberries at him for 5 hours until he finally gave up and left in disgust. People are proud of this town.